DYING

A Psychoanalytic Study with Special Reference to Individual Creativity and Defensive Organization

DYING

*A Psychoanalytic Study with Special Reference to
Individual Creativity and Defensive Organization*

TOR-BJÖRN HÄGGLUND

INTERNATIONAL UNIVERSITIES PRESS, INC.

New York

Library of Congress Cataloging in Publication Data

Hägglund, Tor-Björn.
    Dying.
        Bibliography: p.
        Includes index.
        1. Death—Psychological aspects. 2. Creative
ability. 3. Defense mechanisms. 4. Psychoanalysis.
I. Title.
BF789.D4H26   155.9'37   77-92179
ISBN 0-8236-1510-3

Manufactured in the United States of America

*To Stig, Lasse, Martin, Marianne,
Hannes, Christina, and Anton*

Towards the actual person who has died we adopt a special attitude — something almost like admiration for someone who has accomplished a very difficult task.

— FREUD, "Thoughts for the Times on War and Death"

Contents

Introduction:
Purpose and Method of the Study

My interest in the dying process and the accompanying mourning work stems mainly from two observations that have greatly bewildered me and consequently intrigued me into seeking an explanation for them. The overwhelming feeling of helplessness in the face of death is a self-evident consequence of death's incomprehensible nature, but in addition to the feeling of helplessness and sorrow, the person who loses a beloved one and the dying person himself are both faced with two problems not easily clarified. First of all, they are preoccupied by the inconceivable nature of dying, by the actual process of dying, and then, as a defense against the anxiety of not understanding, they must react either by denying the whole problem or by seeking an answer to it. Already existing patterns of rationalization and the ritualized creativity offered by these patterns provide one answer, or the choice may be a personal solution that uses one's own creative capacity. Speaking of creativity generally, it is usually connected with that part of life which brings something new into the sphere of living, enriching its quality, but the speculations presented in this book concern themselves more with the possibility of approaching death in a creative way, and with the problem of what creativity really is as viewed from this perspective.

Another aspect which bewilders the person who suffers the loss of a near relative, as well as the dying person and the circle

of friends involved, concerns the manner and the content of
discussions about death — in short, how to verbalize the complexity of emotions raised by the experience. The bereaved
person encounters other people's evasive attitudes or their own
personal convictions about death, but seldom is there any true
communication based on observations of the actually dying. It
seems that observations of the dying process and discussions of
it are still subject to some sort of taboo, which in part may be
due to the absence of a common basis of reference for fruitful
communication. To replace this taboo by verbal communication requires a great many detailed case reports about dying
and empathic participation in the dying person's anxieties.

Having abandoned the old lamentations of our particular
culture, which were of great help in the communication between grief-stricken people, we long for something new,
something personal, and something more in keeping with
modern culture to enable us to communicate when we are
confronted with death. One of the goals of this book is to offer
the results obtained during the study of the subject as a step in
the direction of more intimate connectedness when death is to
be met. Time and again while writing this book I have had in
mind the lamentation composed by a six-year-old child in
grief:

Mother — she is in hospital
in her is growing cancer
I myself was born in the summer
I'm cutting lamb's wool
I'll make her a present
it will keep us warm
before Mother's Day she died
to whom can I now give my present.

In contemporary psychiatry, emphasis has been laid on the
significant role of the community, a larger cultural body or the
more limited family culture, in the psychosocial interaction

both in the optimum development of the individual and in the understanding of disturbances. With regard to death, this is as important and central an issue as the two-person relationship. The approach adopted in my study, however, is purely the observation of the two-person relationship. I have attempted to clarify the meaning of the early two-person relationships as well as the psychotherapeutic two-person relationship to the dying individual.

All along the line, psychoanalytic studies of death stress the importance of the two-person relationship to the dying person. In the psychoanalytic literature, denial is commonly referred to as an important ego defense mechanism against fear of death. Frequent references are also made to the importance of transference, especially as a means of relieving the pain of mourning and anxiety as the patient relinquishes all his familiar objects and directs his interest toward the unknown, toward death. My studies of the psychodynamics of dying patients and the artistically creative expression of Edith Södergran's mourning work during her dying process (Part I) brought ego defense mechanisms and their opposite, personal creativity, to my notice, and I believed that it was important to carry on further investigation.

In Part II I have set forth my theoretical conception of dying, of mourning, of phallic-narcissistic defense, and of creativity, based on the literature of this specific field and on my own clinical observations, and placed in the context of the psychoanalytic reference system. In Part III I have applied my theoretical conception to clinical cases, to the dying patients themselves. As a working method I have applied the technique of the psychoanalytic therapeutic alliance with modifications necessitated by the specific problems of the dying patient.

Psychotherapy has been carried out "face to face." Arrangements regarding time have not been strictly adhered to. An average duration was set for the session, but the practice has been to extend the time whenever the patient has shown

signs of unbearable anxiety or fear. In this respect, the purpose
of each session has been to allow the dying patient time enough
to express his actual problems and to attain peace of mind.
Because of the patient's anxiety and fears, it was also necessary
to gratify his need for extra sessions and for contact on the
telephone. Similarly, it has been necessary to comply with the
patient's wishes regarding his helpless physical state that results
from the illness. The patient has received small comforts he
has indicated a wish for, and has been aided in difficulties of
posture, especially toward the end of the dying process: help
has been given in holding a cup or glass for drinking, etc. The
therapist's attitude, especially as death becomes imminent, has
resembled the attitude toward a dependent child. There has
seemed to be no reason to frustrate the dying person in toler-
ating the troubling feelings caused by progressing physical
helplessness; instead, barriers were overcome to offer the
patient a chance to use another person as an object. Another
purpose in the therapy of a dying patient has been to aid him
to use past internalized and present real object relations in
the course of the dying process, and to study this change of
events. In this study I have described the therapeutic process
in detail, with specific emphasis on the transference and the
interaction of the two-person relationship.

My working hypotheses in the study have been the following:

a. Phallic fantasies and the phallic-narcissistic defense
organization are part of the denial of fear of death and fear of
mourning.

b. Phallicity, instead of leading to productive mourning
work, obstructs it. It is not endurable as the dying process
proceeds either, for the fear of loneliness and the fear of
annihilation behind the phallic defense, and the accompanying anxiety and horror, sooner or later overwhelm the dying
patient.

c. Instead, creativity based on the two-person relationship

provides the patient with a solution and lasting relief in the course of the difficult dying process.

d. This kind of creativity can be released for utilization according to the patient's personal abilities in transference, either in the form of creative illusion or of creative activity.

My working hypotheses have only gradually taken form and definite shape (Part I). Especially the studies of Edith Södergran's poetry threw new light on the dying process, on the opposite poles of creativity and defensiveness, in that creativity seeks new libidinal goals, whereas defensiveness keeps to old, beaten tracks in the endeavor to reach a solution. In view of the theoretical aspect on the one hand (Part II), and in the light of clinical cases on the other (Part III), verification of this conception appeared to be important. The answers elicited by my working hypotheses offer a new approach for inspecting, and a wider point of view for recognizing and understanding, the dynamics of the dying process.

PART I

A Study of Loss and Dying, Five Dying Patients, and the Poetry of Edith Södergran

1.

Psychodynamics of the Dying Patient

A REVIEW OF THE LITERATURE

CONCEPTIONS ABOUT THE FEAR OF DEATH

The Unconscious and Death

Death as the absolute cessation of life is beyond the sphere of our experience and being dead is thus an unknown condition. Consequently, studies and opinions of death involve a good deal of information about what death is not, hence something that for various reasons can be excluded. We can recognize death as a fact and as an inescapable event, and accept that the death of other people means losing them forever, but it is hardly likely that anyone can think of his own death as an absolute cessation of all existence. Freud (1915) expressed this in the following way: ". . . the man of prehistoric times survives unchanged in our unconscious. Our unconscious, then, does not believe in its own death; it behaves as if it were immortal" (p. 296).

Klein (1948), on the other hand, assumes that man has unconscious knowledge or understanding that death means a total ending. Jaques (1965) is of the opinion that our unconscious mind in itself has not got an impression about death, but that nevertheless there are a number of unconscious experiences that later on may correspond to a conscious understanding of death. As an example he presents a claustrophobic patient who dreamed that he was lying mutilated in a coffin. In the dream he knew he was dead and was unable to move or to cry. According to Jaques, this dream implies an unconscious fantasy about immobilization and helplessness into which the patient fell as a victim of violent destruction. The fantasy about death in the dream does not, however, correspond to our customary idea of death, because in this dream the patient still maintained his ability to observe what was happening to him. Thus the patient's fantasies and his entering into death merely approach the definitive conscious image of death.

Fear of Death as a Reality

The fear of death in the face of impending death is a phenomenon that seems to be generally observed and accepted in the psychoanalytic literature. In fearing death we are afraid that the thing we have incessantly resisted all our lives is going to happen. Apart from the fear of death's implying the reality of one's own or someone else's death, manifest or overt fear of death may be based on something other than real fear of death or may be imprinted by other sources of anxiety.

According to Stekel (1927-1928), every fear is fundamentally fear of death. Yet the generally held opinion is that death is feared because it signifies separation, loneliness, destruction, chaos, punishment, etc. (Hinton, 1967; Verwoert and Elmore, 1967).

Fear of Death as a Neurotic Phenomenon

As a neurotic phenomenon the fear of death is not actually associated with physical death; instead it has symbolic significance and thus covers other unconscious thoughts. According to Fenichel (1945), such symbolic reflections of death may sometimes have a libidinal character, and death may then indicate, e.g., a reunion with a dead person. Neurotic fear of death mostly veils, however, some childhood sources of anxiety, which later manifest themselves as the fear of death. These sources of anxiety include the fear of losing an object that satisfies important needs, the mother above all, or later, of losing the love and care provided by this important object, the fear of castration, the fear of the superego in the form of a strict, punishing, and forsaking conscience, the fear of one's own masochism which implies the fear of one's own destructive impulses turning toward oneself, and finally, the fear of the superiority of one's own instinctual impulses and the consequent risk of losing control over the ego (Freud, 1923; Waelder, 1960). All these fears may be identified with death and thus may clinically manifest themselves as the fear of death.

The fear of death signifying a fear that a childhood trauma will be repeated may be regarded as a continuous inadequate adaptation to the trauma that did occur. Freud (1926a, 1940) presented a theory of a biological trauma, defining the trauma as a result of the child's inability to deal with his own urgent internal needs, which leads him into a state of helplessness. The prototype of such a biotrauma is birth, a trauma that repeats itself later in various forms involving the loss of the mother or the mother's substitute. Freud presents the hierarchy of various biotraumata: object loss, loss of love, oedipal trauma, etc. According to him, no one escapes them. The weak, immature, and unresisting ego of the small child is unable to deal with things that in later life would not cause any difficulties. In these circumstances both internal instinctual needs and external stimuli may bring about traumata and thus constitute the real background factors of neurotic fear of death.

Adaptation to the Fear of Death

In the light of clinical material, Stern (1968) has claimed that adaptation to death and thinking of death is indispensable for human maturation. Insufficiency in this respect is an

influential factor in the manifestation of neurosis. According
to his theory, the fear of death is generated in early infancy
and at that time constitutes, at bottom, a fear that the previous
biotraumatic situation will recur. Thus the anxiety produced
by a conflict in early infancy is, according to Stern, mixed with
the fear of death in the indefinite future. Clinically this is
manifested by the patient's tending to resort to various infantile symbiotic ways of satisfaction in order to protect himself
against the fear of death and to avoid depression arising from
the fact that it is realized. One acting-out method used here
involves a permanent transference by which the patient fixes
himself in the analytic situation; in other words, the patient
tries to maintain permanent emotional bonds with his analyst
similar to those he had with his mother in early infancy.

Fear of Death in Childhood

The significance of death is not clear to children in spite of
the fact that they employ it a great deal in their play. In
children's games death represents killing and the expression of
aggressive feelings rather than an analysis of the nature of
death: where do they come from and where are they going to.
Freud (1900, p. 254) states that the nature of death is beyond
the child's comprehension; the fear of death as such means
nothing to a child, and children's thoughts are not occupied by
the decomposition of the body, the coldness of the grave, or
eternal nonexistence. For a small child death means merely
leaving on a trip. It is not until the age of five to six years that
the fact that death signifies a final event (Alexander and Adelstein, 1965; Hinton, 1967; Easson, 1968) becomes clear to a
child. Furthermore, even children of school age, who are old
enough to understand the final separation from a dead person,
imagine that physical existence, the only existence known to
them, continues in some form even in death. Proper mourning
at the loss of a deceased person does not make its appearance
until puberty, and even then the real significance of death is

not understood. It is true, though, that, according to Anna Freud (1960, 1967), a child aged three and a half to four years can experience some sort of grief over the loss of a parent.

Crisis Periods of the Fear of Death

Working through the thoughts and fear of death naturally goes on through the entire life and may temporarily be strengthened by extraneous conditions. Yet it has been considered that there are also definite crisis periods in this respect. Jaques (1965) has described the mid-life crisis as one new working through of an infancy depression. The individual's growth toward the peak of physical adulthood ceases in mid-life; he starts growing old and encounters the approach of his own death as a reality. He then goes through a crisis period which now includes an adult insight into one's own death and own destructive impulses or instinctual stimuli. Jaques refers to this crisis as a depressive one, in contrast to the paranoid-schizoid crisis in adolescence, which involves manic opposition to one's own death and strong unconscious denial of one's own destructive instinctual stimuli. "The depressive position" of childhood is gone through qualitatively on another level in middle age. A person's conception of death and the fear involved therein as well as his attitude toward life and work are considerably molded by the result of this working through.

Fear of Death in Old Age

The attitude toward death and the fear of death change in character when one grows old. As physical strength declines and illnesses debilitate one, death may be experienced as a relief (Eissler, 1955; Swenson, 1965), or the fear of death is denied more strongly than ever, which may lead to a paranoid attitude (Christ, 1965). According to Eissler (1955), dying is an easy event in senile dementia, a far progressed aging process, and in this respect comparable to the death of a newborn or quite young baby. He thinks this is associated with the fact that in the beginning of life the death instinct and the life instinct or libidinal instinct have not yet fused and that in old age, on the other hand, life instincts have perhaps discharged all their powers and the death instinct has regained its original dominant position.

FANTASIES OF DEATH

Fantasies of death attempt to fill the gap in our minds created by this unknown condition. In imagination, death is experienced as a trip, punishment, liberator, satisfier of sexual desires, or a condition uniting people. The most usual attitude toward death is acceptance of its inevitability, yet in such a way that its absoluteness as the end of life is simultaneously denied. From time immemorial man has cherished various fantasies of life in the beyond. In many cultures life on earth is believed to be only a part of human existence (Hinton, 1967). Prehistoric man provided the deceased with food, necessary clothing, and weapons. The ancient Egyptians embalmed the bodies to prepare them for life hereafter. Death meant merely a journey or moving from one physical sphere to another. In the religions of primitive cultures death was often described as a voyage across a river or large body of water.

Subsequent cultures accepted physical death as a final separation from the body but declared that life goes on in another kind of eternal form, as a sort of heavenly life or union with the divine monad or a continuous transformation between physical and nonphysical life in the form of reincarnation or rebirth. Religious conceptions strongly support denial of death. Feifel (1959) noted that deeply religious persons deny death and fear of death more strongly than nonreligious people. Firm faith in life after death does not, however, diminish the fear since, in addition to many agreeable promises, it frequently also involves a fear of punishment for moral offenses. The more dependent an individual is on other people, obviously the more intense the denial of the finality of death. In childhood in particular this defense mechanism is total (Stokes, 1966).

Death in itself has also been regarded as a punishment for moral offenses. People talk about deadly sins and a flaming sword guarding Eden, etc. Then either death itself constitutes a punishment or after death will come a punishment that one escaped during one's lifetime. Unconscious oedipal conflicts give rise to fantasies of death of this kind. Death as a punishment signifies the cessation of all bodily "carnal" functions and desires and thus constitutes an equivalent of castration. Myths often describe death as a castrator; e.g., in Karelian mythology death was considered to be a personified figure of some kind who sneaked up on humans (Kemppinen, 1967). It could appear as a nocturnal rider whizzing by, as the Old Reaper, or some other kind of appalling ghost. Omens haunted dreams, and people believed that animals scent death on the move in the neighborhood and express it in various ways; e.g., dogs by howling and wild animals by entering man's quarters. To my mind, beliefs of this kind correspond to fears of punishment that spring from oedipal wishes, hate, and pleasures.

Furthermore, death is often thought to be a relief from life's hardness, thus acquiring a pleasant tone. Apart from the fact that such fantasies involve denial of the fear of death, they also denote a return to a frustrationless condition. Rank (see Munroe, 1955) developed a dualistic conception of the fear of death. Starting from Freud's theory according to which birth constitutes the prototype of biotrauma, he presented a generalized dualism. He proposed that on the one hand the person struggles to free himself from bonds and to become independent, which is life's essential aim, but on the other he desires to return to the sheltering womb and to be blended with the surrounding world. In this connection Rank referred to a primary fear of death, which implies a much more primitive fear of losing oneself, disappearing and merging into a larger unity. Thus this fear is different from the empirical fear of death of which each of us has heard when still quite a child.

McClelland (1964) has described how death may be experienced as a threatening father, obscene old man, or old prostitute. He has also observed that death is experienced as a harlequin, gay seducer, and passionate lover. Death being libidinized or sexualized in this way is, according to his observations, more common in females than in males, in whom the fear of castration prevents the generation of such fantasies (Papageorgis, 1966). A corresponding idea is reflected in various phrases referring to death: fiction employs such expressions as the kiss of death, the lap of death, surrendering to death, etc. (Greenberger, 1965).

Bromberg and Schilder (1936) have described how neurotic women's fantasies of death often include imagining death as some kind of reunion with the ideal love object which does not exist in real life but which becomes permissible after death. The forbidden and lost incestuous object is thus regained in death. Fantasies about being a bride of Christ are probably involved in visions of this kind. One of my female patients (case 4, see below) repeatedly dreamed, and later before her death hallucinated, about a man who "radiated love" and kept sitting in her room waiting for her.

According to Greenberger (1965), the unusually easy death of many women, unperplexed by any considerable worries about the future, is associated with feminine passivity as well as with a greater tendency in women to libidinize death.

Both Freud (1926a) and Waelder (1960) observed that a child's separation from the mother and maternal love provokes separation anxiety which is later manifested as symbolic fear of death. Fantasies seeking to reduce this separation anxiety are conceptions that death is a condition or an event uniting people, e.g., a divine monad, post-mortem paradise, or visions of the deceased passing over to his dead relatives or fore-fathers. According to Eissler (1955), this is a frequent phenomenon, especially when the spouse or the parents have died earlier.

THE DYING PATIENT

Denial of Death

When an individual must face his own death and comprehends that it is a real development to occur in the near future, deep changes are naturally bound to take place in him. In order to bridle his fear within endurable confines he regresses (F. Deutsch, 1935), and in the course of the regressive process his defense mechanisms strengthen and are possibly transformed into a more archaic form resembling those of early infancy.

Case histories that describe the psychodynamics of dying patients are relatively few. Felix Deutsch (1935), Eissler (1955), Sandford (1957), Joseph (1962), and Norton (1963) have published such cases. All the patients described were dying of cancer. Freud (1915) and Eissler (1955) refer to the reluctance to being in contact with a dying person, and this may be a factor contributing to the rarity of such case reports. These researchers emphasize the significance of a psychotherapeutic attitude and how important it is to learn to understand better the psychodynamics of a dying patient.

A person runs away from the reality of death by availing himself of various defense mechanisms. Society offers ready rationalization patterns in philosophical and religious systems (Wahl, 1965), which are often characterized by magic and regression. A person's first reaction and attempt to manage the intolerable prospect of death is to deny the danger, either partially or entirely.

Other ego defense mechanisms gain importance in proportion as denial begins to fail. In this respect denial is highly dependent on the person's stage of development, being, e.g., complete in childhood, and on the degree of regression brought about by the progressive process of dying.

Denial of hard realities has been considered a precursor of the ego defense mechanisms, but it has also been called the most primitive and stable defense mechanism (Altschul, 1968). It is in this sense that its significance as the principal defense mechanism in the face of impending death may be understood (Browne and Hackett, 1967). Denial of death may have a multigrade character. All ideas about its reality may be denied on the fantasy level, its significance to the person or its time may be denied, and so on. Denial may even develop into psychotic forms, in which case death as a reality or the existence of the disease is denied altogether. The deeper the regression the poorer the sense of reality, and thus denial as a mechanism of reducing the fear of death is reinforced as the process of dying progresses and the regression becomes deeper. In the final stage hallucinatory features may appear (Eissler, 1955; Norton, 1963), the patient hallucinating, according to the pleasure principle, about pleasant memories of his life or about his immortality.

Work of Mourning

In waiting for death the patient goes through the work of mourning. In the usual work of mourning libidinal energy fixed on the lost object is released and can be attached to another object. The lost objects of a dying patient include, in addition to emotionally important persons, his own body. According to Eissler (1955), by the gradual work of mourning the dying patient decathects the objects, including his own body, and thus when the moment of death closes in his concern and libido are withdrawn from the world. This facilitates the process of accepting death, a natural result of the libidinal energy's constellation at that moment. The patient cannot achieve this, however, if no substitute is available to fill the place of the lost object. Another person, e.g., somebody taking a psychotherapeutic attitude toward the patient, or the patient's various fantasies, may provide a substitute object in this sense. According to Eissler, deeply religious patients may endure their work of mourning by withdrawing from the world and other persons, and by transferring the released libidinal interests to their fantasy about God and existence after death.

The patient Norton (1963) describes found during her work of mourning, through transference, her therapist a suitable object for her released libido, and was certain that they belonged together even in death. My patients were to a great degree occupied by recollections and fantasies of dead relatives with whom they had had positive connections and whom they had earlier mourned to a certain extent. It is my opinion that such a recollection of mother, spouse, or some other deceased person can be recathected with the released libido. Such a recathected memory as an object may be the very transference object; e.g., patients 3 and 4 (see below) created an intense maternal transference toward me. On the other hand, they cherished fantasies about how they would go to mother when they died. They had combined the love objects of life and death with each other.

Developing a Surviving Auxiliary Ego

Pfister (1930) observed that when certain persons suddenly run into great danger of losing their lives, their thoughts return to earlier childhood situations in which such dangers were overcome. Thereafter they proceed to think about the future, and it may be possible to achieve pleasant hallucinatory visions about a successful future. The sequence runs rapidly, and the visions change as in a movie. According to Eissler (1955), in these cases the ego seems to construct a new personality in the face of deadly danger by re-experiencing dangerous situations which were successfully overcome in the past and by imagining a favorable future. When, in such a reconstruction process, the ego reaches the present, which implies the danger, it deviates from the current reality and successfully moves over from the past into a safe future.

Eissler (1955) and Norton (1963) observed a similar mechanism in the cases they describe. In their thoughts the patients provided the persons who were bound to take care of their children and duties with the excellent properties of their own egos, thus creating new egos. In addition, they generated illusions of egos that would maintain their object relationships and consequently they could unfasten their bonds with these objects.

Conflict between Hate and Devotion

A very essential point in the psychodynamics of a dying person is the solution of his own ambivalent, antagonistic, and contradictory emotions. For death signifies not only giving up objects but also being given up and forsaken by relatives. Without a substitute this provokes hate and anxiety in him. It has been observed (F. Deutsch, 1935) that, in order to avoid the anxiety and hostile feelings toward relatives brought about by this ambivalence, a dying patient sometimes endeavors to strengthen his devotion by clinging to them, so that he is able to die calmly only in their presence.

Ambivalent feelings are reciprocal, of course. It has, indeed, been thought that the feelings of guilt that arise from the aggressive elements of the ambivalence between the dying patient and his relatives generally prevent relatives from treating, in a psychotherapeutic sense, the one who is approaching death. According to Eissler, the aggressive aspect of one's own ambivalence is an essential contributing factor to the tendency of relatives to avoid the dying patient. The same basic difficulty also applies to the therapist and, more generally, to all those who treat dying patients. There is a difference, however, in that the positive aspect of the patient's ambivalence is in a greater degree turned to the therapist (Norton, 1963), and in that the therapist does not mobilize mourning and defense mechanisms against it to an equal degree.

Hope of Immortality

This natural ambivalence (Eissler, 1955) constitutes a great burden to the dying patient as he aspires, by his work of mourning, to provide his libido with an object relationship that is as free as possible from aggressions and the guilt and anxiety involved in them. The therapist's greater freedom from guilt enhances the possibility of his constituting such an object for the patient and of affording him the emotions he needs in this situation. According to Eissler, these emotions include sympathy, care, and confidence that something in the patient is immortal. Thus the therapist can demonstrate to the dying patient that he is not alone but belongs to someone, in this way alleviating his fear of separation.

Patients with a religious conviction find their immortality in it. Levin (1964) has discussed immortality and presented certain realistic points of view that apply to every dying patient. They involve the patient's own identity and the existing evidence that proves he has lived. These may comprise his children, work, property—everything he leaves behind after his death. The patient may even gain a feeling of immortality from the knowledge that he will live in other people's memories, and in this respect too the therapist's role is important.

Distribution of Hate and Love

When death results from an illness the threat mobilizes instinctual energy, and concern is directed to the illness (Joffe and Sandler, 1967). According to Felix Deutsch (1935), libido is withdrawn from objects when the body is threatened by an illness and turned instead to the diseased organ. All such dangers of illness are experienced as extraneous threats of punishment, and this aggression, affecting the ego, launches a defensive ego reaction. The defense may manifest itself as increased aggression toward the outer world or as self-directed masochistic suffering. The more clearly the disease progresses into inevitable danger with no escape and no means of defense, the more intensely the ego feels it is losing, and the fear of death correspondingly increases. Finally, a flight into a psychosis is often the only possible outcome. In such a case the patient may, in his thoughts, take the disease as an actual personal enemy or persecutor. This may lead to the development of paranoia and a severe depression or melancholy when the threat is experienced as issuing from the superego. Practically, this manifests itself as a paranoid attitude toward relatives and those who are treating the patient, or as frantic self-accusations, confessions of offenses, and apologies. In this way aggressive and libidinal instinctual energies are directed to other objects, both tending to gain strength or satisfaction, and in this sense even the own body constitutes an object.

The ego of a dying patient undergoes a split in the way that libidinal and aggressive feelings seek different objects. In patient 1 in my material (see below) this manifested itself in his establishing a very regressive positive relationship with me. He experienced me as a good mother and us as an alliance, in stark contrast to the outside world, where he saw hate between relatives and observed that man pollutes nature and destroys animals; in death he would be relieved of these destructive forces of mankind.

The sharp split in the ego of a dying patient into good and bad during the regressive state preceding his death has an analogy in early infancy. Klein's (1948) theory of depression implies the concept of a "depressive position" into which the baby enters during the first six months of his life. Before that, during the very first months, when he has only partial objects, the child solves his anxiety by dividing the object, the breast, into good and bad, which corresponds to the ego split into a loving and hating portion. According to Jaques (1965), a person's unconscious attitude toward death depends on this split and on how he has worked through the "depressive position" in infancy. According to Winnicott (1954), the mother serves as an object for the child's aggressions during states of instinctual pressure and, correspondingly, for love when the child is satisfied. The source of guilt is the fact that those two emotions become united in the object. The bipartition of the ego during a dying patient's regression possibly removes the guilt brought about by the ambivalence. In certain cases this has been observed as a sudden brightening, a feeling of a miracle of some kind, the conflict of ambivalence suddenly disappearing at the same time. Evil is left behind, good things are present and ahead. Sandford (1952, 1957) has described how an obsessional patient in psychoanalysis died of pulmonary carcinoma. The patient's difficulty lay in the problem of how to solve his ambivalent emotions; he accomplished this by dividing himself and his mother image into two, into an external attending portion, "the good breast," and an internal "bad cancer breast." When he experienced that evil had been totally cut off from him he lived through such a miracle, in which everything was good and signified a union with the "ideal mother."

Introjection of the Therapist

Norton (1963) has described the process of transference in a woman dying of breast cancer. In the beginning phase, during the work of mourning, a strong affection for the therapist developed which, when associated with a need to create a relationship with as little ambivalence as possible, provided the patient with a possibility to re-externalize her superego, i.e., to get rid of the demands of her moral ego by substituting for them imaginary expectations from the therapist. The patient also identified herself with her positive emotions toward the therapist and repeated some aspects of her relationship to the mother in her infancy. Later she experienced the therapist as a portion of her own ego, one kind of "auxiliary ego" that took care of her well-being. Any threat of losing the therapist excited infantile separation anxiety. Regression reached a level where the boundaries between the object and the subject were occasionally vague: the patient experienced that the therapist was constantly present and hallucinated about their union even in her death.

In the case of two patients in my material our union in death appeared in their last verbal expressions. One of them (case 3) hallucinated that we were walking together on a meadow, the day being like one of those sunny days in childhood. The other (case 4) had hallucinations about a car that was waiting to carry us away together. Here, too, the final stage was introjection of the therapist.

SUMMARY

The principal defense mechanism against the fear of death is denial; only after it fails do other mechanisms, especially the more primitive defense mechanisms, projection and introjection, come into prominence. The dynamic aspect of the dying process is influenced by the working through of the separation anxiety in infancy as well as by the whole lifelong working through of separation and death, which possibly attains its most clear-cut form in the so-called mid-life crisis.

Figure 1 illustrates certain important features in the psychodynamics of a dying patient. The threat of impending death is at first met with denial of the danger in one form or another. When denial fails the work of mourning begins, leading the person to give up life and his own body. Simultaneously the dying patient expresses wishes for immortality, e.g., by developing some other person as his "auxiliary ego"

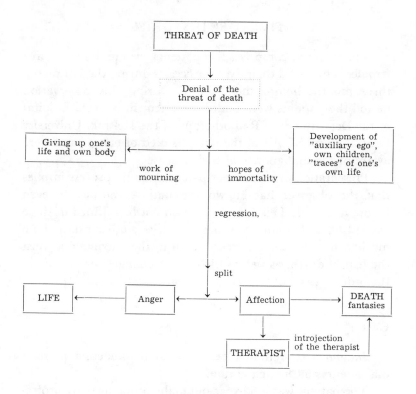

FIGURE 1

A schematic illustration of the psychodynamics of the dying patient

that will survive, or by experiencing his immortality as lying in his children or in his achievements in life.

When denial of impending death fails, the ego regresses and the emotions split into hate and love, into an evil and a good world. Hate is directed and projected into life and one's own body, which the dying patient has got to give up. Affection is attached to the fantasies he has about death and to the transference to the therapist, whom the patient subsequently joins with himself through introjection, experiencing with him a union in death.

FIVE CASE HISTORIES

The material comprises five patients, two males and three females; I observed their dying processes during the last one to three months before their death. During this observation period the patients were under treatment in Koskela hospital or the Department of Radiotherapy of the Helsinki University Central Hospital. All of the patients died of cancer and were aware of the malignancy of their disease.

Presentation of a coherent psychodynamic process implies that the observer has known the patient thoroughly even before he fell ill. This condition could not be fulfilled in these cases. I have therefore confined myself to studying only those mechanisms the patients resorted to in their struggle against the fear of death, as well as the psychic changes discernible in them during the time preceding death.

CASE 1

Diagnosis: Carcinoma hepatocellulare, anaemia perniciosa, aneurysma luetica aortae.

The patient was a 69-year-old male, a manager by profession. At the age of about 20 he had suffered from syphilis. Three years before his death he was discovered to suffer from an aortic aneurysm and pernicious anemia. Hepatic carcinoma was diagnosed in him four months before his death. The patient was immediately apprised of the malignancy of the disease. The diagnosis was confirmed by needle biopsy. Neither operation nor radiotherapy was considered expedient; palliative treatment was resorted to. The progress of the carcinomatous process in the liver was rapid. Metastases were not found. The primary neoplasm constituted the immediate cause of death.

The patient lived with his wife and two adult children and had been working until he became ill. Thereafter he was in outpatient treatment for one and a half months, still living at home. His immediate reaction to the illness was depression and a clinging appeal to his relatives "since he would soon die." In his communications he often repeated the sentence: "I won't ever see another summer." The patient then gave up talking about death, concentrating on treating himself by carefully following the prescriptions of drug administration and by attempting to improve his condition by eating properly. At the same time, however, he noticed that he was losing weight and worried about this. He was convinced that the physicians had been mistaken about the diagnosis. He believed that he suffered from cirrhosis of the liver and that he could cure it by eating quantities of the right foods. During his last days at home he had frightening visual hallucinations although the sense of reality remained unaffected. He saw on the ceiling small creatures that were subsequently transformed into worms. The hallucinations appeared at the same time that he could no longer sit up in bed.

When the patient was admitted to the hospital he was bedridden, in poor condition, and his liver was greatly enlarged. Yet his thoughts and ability to make contacts were still intact. He was willing to talk, trusting in me as an attachment from the very beginning. He never asked me about the nature of his disease nor for any opinions about his life expectancy. He continuously looked for signs of improvement in himself, in this way attempting to deny the progress of the disease. He tried to please me and the ward staff by being "a contented patient."

Five weeks before his death the fear of death suddenly burst out in a fierce way. A pronounced psychic regression occurred in him. He emphasized that he had been doing his best to satisfy everyone and still they were now angry with him and wanted to harm him. "All my life I have been trying my best, even now I have kept eating but I'm losing weight just the same, I haven't strength enough to grab a glass of milk, now

I'm too weak even to try." At this time the patient was extremely anxious, cried, and begged God for mercy. He sought to obtain close contact by taking me by the hand, and he assured me that since he had always been helped in life's critical situations he would be helped now, too.

One week before his death he poured forth his wrath intensely, first directing it toward various objects such as the headphone of the hospital radio, then toward the ward personnel, blaming them for neglecting and disturbing him. Later on he considered that other people are normally evil, wanting to exclude them: "I don't care to learn about the badness of the world, jukebox noise and debauched youth. Young people are just after selfish satisfaction of their lusts. The badness of mankind is going to destroy the world. New inventions are employed to exterminate life, little creatures are poisoned and polluted lakes kill the fish."

Two days before his death he had completely located the "evil" world that he was going to abandon, he was free from anxiety, and felt in comfortable safety: "Christ is waiting for me and I'm going to get rest." He expressed intense affection toward me, being certain that we would meet again in death. For the last 12 hours of his life he was in coma.

Summary of Case 1

The patient's attitude toward the malignancy of his illness was a short-term fear of death. He then denied in his mind that his illness was malignant, incurable, and progressive, and that he could not be helped. When the denial mechanism failed and his general condition continued to deteriorate, the fear of death suddenly emerged into consciousness and he underwent a psychic regression. He began to accentuate his kindness, subsequently directing and projecting his hostility toward people who would survive him. The success of this projection brought him great relief. In this way he himself gave up evil, while the good as well as his affection for the therapist were located in the future beyond his death. In his imagination he regarded death as a peaceful retreat where the dead meet each other.

CASE 2

Diagnosis: Carcinoma ventriculi, emphysema pulmonum.

The patient was a former painter on pension, 71 years old. He had suffered from pulmonary emphysema for more than 20 years. Three months before his death a carcinoma of the ventricle was discovered. Symptoms had appeared about six months earlier but the patient did not consult a doctor at that time. The patient resolutely opposed any surgical operations, which therefore were not resorted to. X-ray examinations revealed a large tumor in the cranial portion of the ventricle. The neoplasm had infiltrated a large area of the wall of the ventricle. By the time of admission to the hospital the patient was emaciated and in poor condition. Radiotherapy was not administered, his treatment being of a merely palliative nature. The immediate cause of death was the primary neoplasm.

The patient was single. All his life he had lived as a subtenant or in workers' settlements. He had made his living mainly as a painter and as a sailor, but during the last years he had been living on welfare assistance, residing in a dormitory. His nearest relative was a sister with whom he had very infrequent contacts. Apart from his sister the patient had no permament relationships with people. In his earlier days the patient had used alcohol profusely and changed jobs frequently, nevertheless working until the age when he became entitled to a pension.

The patient was willing to have contact and to talk, but he did not appeal for anyone's aid. He reacted to his illness by denying its malignancy. He was afraid of surgical operations but, on the other hand, he did not express any fear of death.

He directed his attention and hopes of recovery to "good food" and medication. He wanted to please the ward personnel in order to secure the administration of medicine.

The patient's attitudes toward the nursing personnel and me remained the same through the hospitalization period. He asked for drugs, in general both analgesics and such medicines as, according to his hopes, would cure him. When surgical operations were suggested, he refused categorically, became reticent, and threatened to leave the hospital.

The nursing personnel did not receive either his anger or his affection, but about two weeks before his death, when he could no longer sit up in bed unaided, he began to recall memories of his parents. He dreamed about his father's being drunk and raging, and he directed his wrath to memories of his father. In his recollections his mother was tender and took good care of him. When, during his last days, the patient talked about his mother he often suddenly fell asleep. Before he died he was unconscious for two days.

Summary of Case 2

The patient had been living without permanent contacts except those of his childhood family. As an adult, the use of alcohol served as an important means of releasing anxiety. He reacted to his illness by denying its malignancy. He was assured that there were medicines that would cure him. He refused surgical operations as he was afraid of them, but the fear of death did not reach consciousness, owing to intense denial supported by a strong belief that drugs provided safety and were pharmacologically effective. During his last days he used his good memories of his mother to suppress fear and anxiety, while his anger was directed toward the memory of his father.

CASE 3

Diagnosis: Carcinoma overaii cum carcinosis peritonei, myodegeneratio et insufficientia cordis, dementia senilis.

The patient was a former seamstress, 79 years of age. For 10 years she had suffered from mild cardiac insufficiency. Laparotomy revealed the patient's tumor nine months before her death: there were abundant small metastases all over the peritoneum, especially in the pelvic parts and in omentum and mesenterium. Biopsy of the omentum confirmed the histological diagnosis as carcinoma partim papillare, partim adenomatosum, the structure suggesting ovarian carcinoma. The patient did not undergo an operation, nor was radiotherapy administered to her. The primary tumor and the abdominal metastases constituted the immediate cause of death.

The patient had been left a widow 20 years before. She had two adult children who came to see her only very infrequently. The patient had lived in an old people's home for five years, where she behaved restlessly and manifested hostile attitudes toward the nursing staff. Her memory had deteriorated, and she suspected others in a paranoid manner when her memory failed. During the last years she had received small doses of chlorprothixen.

When admitted to the hospital the patient was confused and restless. These symptoms were intensified after she had been operated on, making conversation with her impossible. The confusion lasted for two weeks. During this time her general condition and fluid balance improved. The patient's psychiatric medication consisted of butaperazin and pericyazin. She was now able to communicate, and she could be out of bed for a short time each day. Her medication was changed into chlorpromazine, 50 to 100 mg daily, remaining so until the end.

The patient assumed an accusing and hostile attitude toward her children and the nursing staff. She accused them of neglecting and harming her and of wishing her to die. In the beginning she had a similar attitude toward me, too, but when she found her medicines suitable for her she began to praise them, and thereafter, for a month before her death, she developed an affection toward me and longed for our daily sessions. Her negative attitude toward the hospital staff and her children grew still stronger and she tried to avoid them.

Two weeks before her death she asked for the first time if the illness was malignant. She had not been told earlier. She seemed, however, to have guessed the severity of her illness and she took the information about cancer with no great affect. Thereafter she often repeated the sentence: "Some people die, others are allowed to live." She began to be suspicious about who she was, often asking me about that. At the same time she saw in me various features of her own mother, laying particular emphasis on the similarity of the eyes. She kept inquiring where her childhood home was. She thought that her mother had died only recently and said she was going to her. Simultaneously she asked me to be with her and to depart with her from this life. During her last days a confusional state developed, with hallucinations about how we were walking together on a warm and sunny meadow of her childhood. She then expressed the belief that I was her mother. Here verbal contact between us came to an end; the patient was unconscious for about 12 hours before she died.

Summary of Case 3

The patient, who before falling ill with cancer harbored a paranoid attitude and suffered from forgetfulness due to senility, was not certain about the malignancy of her illness. She was hostile and combative toward everybody. Drug therapy made it possible to create a therapeutic contact with her, after which she began to direct her affection toward the therapist while the feelings of hatred were directed elsewhere. The division of feelings calmed her so that she was able to make it clear for herself that her illness was malignant. Furthermore, she was able to experience fear of death. Hatred was directed toward the world that had to be given up, while affection was attached to the mother and the therapist, whom she identified with her mother. Through introjection she combined these two objects into one, thus avoiding the fear of being left alone.

CASE 4

Diagnosis: Carcinoma mammae sin. cum metastatibus hepatis, pulmonum et lymphonodorum colli.

The patient was a 36-year-old housewife who previously had been in good health. A tumor was discovered in her left breast 18 months before her death. The histological diagnosis was carcinoma ductale mammae. A radical operation was performed after which she was administered radiotherapy. Thereafter the patient had no symptoms for more than a year. Four months before her death hepatic metastases were found. The metastatic growth progressed rapidly in spite of radiotherapy and bilateral ovariotomy. One month before death metastases were found in the lungs and a little later in the lymphatic glands in the neck. Death resulted from the hepatic metastases.

The patient had a husband and school-age children. She was under home treatment except during the operation period and the last three months of her life, when she was hospitalized. She was informed of the malignancy of her illness as soon as the diagnosis was made. She reacted to this information with fear and anxiety that lasted for a couple of days. Later on she believed that the treatment would cure her. One year after the operation, before the hepatic metastases had been discovered, she was convinced that she would recover. The patient's reaction to the metastases was depression: she felt that her "days of grace" had now come to an end. She concentrated on treating herself by strictly following the doctor's advice, and attached particular importance to nutrition, forcing herself to eat foods she did not like in the belief that their nutritional value would promote her convalescence.

She became aware of the fear of death when the rupture of esophageal varices resulted in a massive hemorrhage six weeks before her death. In that connection she was in coma for some 12 hours, had felt she was dying, and when she regained consciousness was uncertain whether she was alive or dead. The fear of death and anxiety called forth deep psychic regression in her, as a result of which she began to seek security and protection in me. She experienced me as a mother feeding and soothing her, and expressed these feelings verbally.

After recovering from the hemorrhage she could be out of bed some of the time; the regressive attitude persisted, however. Her interest in her children began to diminish. At first she stifled her feelings, took the photographs of her children off the table, and made them visit her less often. Finally she no longer talked about her children, as she felt that they were properly taken care of. This stage had been preceded by her personally selecting a nursemaid for them, insisting that the children be brought up carefully according to her directions. In this way, through another person, she had the sensation of taking care of them.

As her interest in her children diminished, memories of her own childhood streamed into her mind. The memories involved especially her affection toward her own mother, who had died of cancer 13 years before. She offered many recollections of what her mother had expected her to achieve, and explained that she had met her mother's wishes. In terms of her illness she identified herself with her mother, commenting with satisfaction on how well she could now understand various details of her mother's illness as they were at present manifest in herself.

The patient thus directed her affection toward good memories of her mother and toward me, regarding me as a mother for her. Her anger, on the other hand, she poured forth on one nurse in particular, whom she accused of mercilessly torturing her, as well as on certain relatives whom she thought were rejoicing at her illness.

By this time, two weeks before her death, the patient could no longer sit up in bed unaided. She dreamed repeatedly that there was a man in her room sitting on a chair and waiting for her. A couple of days before her death she had hallucinations about the same illusion. In the beginning this man was sometimes "dark and terrifying," sometimes "light and amicable." One week before her death she had a relieving feeling that "the dark man" had vanished and that the man present was always "good and radiating love."

Henceforth the patient grew indifferent to the outside world. Most of the time she slept, hoping then that I would be present. She indicated that she sought in me maternal love and protection, combining her fantasies of me with the memories of her own mother. She believed firmly that she would again meet her mother in one form or another after her death.

On the last day of her life she lost her sense of reality. She was restless but not agitated; she tried to get up, insisting that I help her, and kept prompting me: "We must hurry, we've got to leave on a trip right away and there's a car waiting for us." She experienced that we were going together. This was the last verbal contact between us; she lay unconscious less than 24 hours before she died.

Summary of Case 4

In the beginning the patient repressed her fear of death by denying the poor results of the treatment and by cherishing a belief that it was successful. The breakthrough of the fear of death resulted in a deep psychic regression. her emotional interest was diverted from the habitual sphere and concern of her life; she tried to fill the gap with a person whom she instructed and supplied with her own conceptions. Her interest was displaced to a dead person, her mother, to whom she thought she was going. Through displacement of emotions she experienced the therapist as a protective mother. The split in emotions manifested itself in her attaching her affection to

what was ahead while directing her anger to what had to be
given up. Introjection of the therapist, taking him along with
her in death, came as the final development.

CASE 5

Diagnosis: Carcinoma ventriculi cum metastatibus hepatis et cavi abdominis.

The patient was an 83-year-old widow whose husband had
been a truck gardener. She had previously enjoyed good
health. Three months before death laparotomy revealed a
widely infiltrated tumor in the ventricle with extremely abundant metastatic growth all over the intestinal tract and the
liver. The histological diagnosis was carcinoma cirrhosum.
Surgical removal of the neoplasm was not attempted, nor was
the patient administered radiotherapy. The primary neoplasm
and the metastases in the abdominal cavity were the immediate cause of death.

In spite of her abdominal symptoms the patient had hesi-
tated for three months before consulting a doctor. At first she
opposed surgical explorations and any potential operations.
Right up until her death she refused analgesics.

The patient had been left a widow three years earlier when
her husband died of pulmonary carcinoma. She had two adult
children, both of whom were married. She lived alone, but
spent the period of her illness with her daughter's family,
except for the exploratory phase and the last month of her life
when she was under treatment in the hospital. The malignancy
of the disease had been explained to her right after the examinations. She received the information quite calmly, stating
that she had been expecting something like that and that it was
now her turn to die off.

The patient talked with me as well as with her relatives very
composedly and directly. Her thoughts ran smoothly and her
memory was clear. She ate and drank very little. She did not

find herself in need of any closer contact. She reacted to her slight pains by remarking that they would pass off. She objected to analgesics, considering them unnecessary. She did not take any interest in possible signs indicating recovery; on the contrary, she observed the progress of the illness, figuring out how soon she would die.

The patient was convinced that there is life after death and that after she had departed this world she would meet her late husband. She was not afraid of death; quite the opposite, she was longing for it, and her interest was mainly attached to fantasies of life beyond death. The patient's death was not preceded by a state of unconsciousness.

Summary of Case 5

By means of the working through of the mourning involving the loss of her husband, the patient had in her mind denied that she had finally lost her husband and she was certain that, owing to her age, she would soon die and rejoin him. In this sense death did not mean to the patient surrendering important emotional objects but, on the contrary, implied regaining them. Denial of the meaning of death was manifested even to the extent that she did not think of the meaning of the destruction of her own body, denying its importance. As the mechanisms of denial were effective she did not develop a fear of death or psychic regression, which would have demanded mobilization of different ego defense mechanisms.

DISCUSSION OF THE CASES

The patients presented here differ a great deal from one another in personal problems, personality characteristics, and social background. It could therefore be expected that the patients' attitudes toward death would vary in personal terms from one to another.

The patients' fantasies about death manifest denial of

death as a final event either on the basis of religious conviction (case 1) or through the conception that death is a condition where one can unite with previously lost relatives, such as mother (cases 3 and 4) or spouse (case 5). In one patient (case 2) the absence of corresponding fantasies may have been associated with the use of alcohol or drugs, which served as a substitute for his need for contacts with other people, both in reality and in fantasies. One of the female patients (case 4) for some time cherished an eroticized and personified image of death awaiting her — and in fact she was the only patient of fertile age. An aged, lonely female patient (case 5) experienced that death was going to liberate her from loneliness. She was the only one who at no stage of her dying process manifested overt fear of death. No one of the patients directly interpreted death as punishment, but this interpretation was manifested indirectly in the way they believed that obedience, submission, and proper eating would lengthen life (cases 1, 2, and 4).

The patients' fantasies of death were not permanent but changed as regression grew deeper; e.g., in the fantasies of one female patient (case 4) death was at first a punisher who allowed her a time of grace, then a personified frightful figure, later a man radiating love, and finally, as regression went still deeper, she experienced death as an awaiting mother with whom she was going to unite.

In order to dispel the fear of death, all the patients employed denial as a defense. As denial failed (cases 1 and 4) intense fear of death emerged, followed by a psychic regression. It is possible that denying the risk and threatening death is characteristic of patients who have fallen ill with cancer, in which the likelihood of dying is, according to common knowledge, greater than in many other diseases. Achté and Vauhkonen (1967a, 1967b) have observed that denial of the risk is a common defense mechanism in patients with cancer, even if there is no immediate risk of death.

An essential concern in the patients' work of mourning

involved finding new objects for released emotions. The patients directed their affection toward fantasies of what was ahead (cases 1, 3, 4, and 5) while anger was poured on what had to be given up (cases 1 and 3). When the splitting of emotions did not occur in this way, a need to seek separate objects for affection and anger was still discernible. Where the splitting of emotions occurred the patient got rid of a great deal of anxiety (cases 1, 3, and 4) associated with the guilt brought about by the ambivalence. The therapist constituted an object for the affection of these patients (cases 1, 3, and 4) and thus he effected a reduction of the fear of separation. These patients experienced an alliance with the therapist when they died, and through introjection they felt his presence in death.

SUMMARY

The psychiatric and psychoanalytic literature on dying is reviewed, and the author's own experience with the psychodynamics of the dying patient is described. The subject is treated from the points of view of the fear of death and the fantasies of death exhibited by the dying patient. The need of the dying patient for supportive psychotherapy is discussed. Five case reports are given.

2.

A Psychoanalytic Approach to the Creativity and the Mourning Work in the Poetry of Edith Södergran

WOMAN AND CREATIVITY

THE VERY PERSONAL

In a broad sense productive and creativity activity can be viewed as an attempt to influence and transform already existing outer reality and the flow of actual events. In the individual mind the conception of external realities is focused on subjective understanding and totally personal striving. From this point of view creative activity becomes an act of recreating what already exists but is not found to be in harmony with the person's inner subjective experience.

The generally accepted and conventional conceptions of art and scientific work are confronted by those of a most personal and individual kind. Milner (1957) points out that the creative artist "may contribute to this convention ..., enrich and enlarge it, but he cannot start off without it, he cannot jump off from nothing" (p. 134). Modell (1970) also empha-

---

Co-authored with Mikael Enckell.

sizes the importance of the environment and existing traditions in a broader sense in the act of creating by saying:

> What is created is not an entirely new environment but a *transformation* of that which already exists. This suggests that an essential element of creativity is an *acceptance* of that which is outside the self. This acceptance implies some mastery of the attitude of primitive ambivalence toward the original (maternal) object . . . true creativity, whether in art or science, also requires the acceptance of a prior tradition which stands for the nonself that is transformed by the creative art [pp. 244-245].

When creative work is more concerned with convention and does not allow the emergence of the self, the act of creation has a ritualized form. Modell (1970) has compared the art creations of prehistoric man with Winnicott's concept of the transitional object, calling attention to some important differences. The spontaneous individual product found in children's creative play does not occur in the art creations of prehistoric man. In his artistic work primitive man tried to avoid completely a purely personal touch, resorting instead to the use of universal symbols, which usually took the form of animals. For example, the human face or head was hardly ever depicted; rather, a more common symbol, that of an animal head, was substituted. Modell contends that prehistoric art was not an expression of individual creation but rather part of a religious ritual. The productive artist as such was only an instrument in the hands of a rigidly constrained religious tradition. Artists were magicians endowed with a special gift, but their creative work had become ritualized in the same way that a modern priest carries on the services and mass in church. In religious rituals, as in some very typical academic proceedings for that matter, the creative process has become strictly ritualized and is more intent on the acquisition of a position of power than on providing an outlet for individual creative talent, whereas the individual creative process has the more constant aim of achieving a balance between purely personal inspiration and the legacy of convention. It is an effort to overcome an obstacle not by ritual control, but by gaining mastery, by remolding and recreating one's own personal understanding of and compassion for others.

WINNICOTT'S TRANSITIONAL OBJECT AND CREATIVITY

Winnicott's discovery that there is a close relationship between the creative artist and the beholder of the work of art in their mutual attitude toward the created product led him to make observations on the transitional object. He explains (1953) that the transitional object and the transitional phenomenon are the child's first creative relationship with his environment. The child draws a picture of an inanimate object and has the sensation of importance, but the process is not merely psychic nor is the created object hallucinatory. The transitional object is a part of the environment, a part to be found by the child whenever the need arises. This is the area between oral erotism and real object relations, between primary creative activity and the projection of something already introjected. The child experiences the transitional object not as part of himself, but as part of something the self has created through a self-conceived illusory picture. It is a personal illusion linked to a concrete object or to something that has really happened. Gradually the transitional object becomes unnecessary as real object relations grow stronger, and the child is able to give it up without the mourning work that follows the loss of real objects.

According to Winnicott, the illusion of the transitional object and the transitional phenomenon are inherent in children's play, in adult creative work, in beholding a work of art, etc. Here lies the basis of all creativity activity. Winnicott (1971) says that

The creative impulse is therefore something that can be looked at as a thing in itself, something that of course is necessary if an artist is to produce a work of art, but also as something that is present when anyone — baby, child, adolescent, adult, old man or woman — looks in a healthy way at anything or does anything deliberately, such as making a mess with feces or prolonging the act of crying to enjoy a musical sound. It is present as much in the moment-by-moment living of a backward child who is enjoying breathing as it is in the inspiration of an architect who suddenly knows what it is that he wishes to construct, and who is thinking in terms of material that can actually be used so that his creative impulse may take form and shape, and the world may witness [p. 69].

It is well known that creativity plays an important part in loss and mourning. The pain that follows loss of an important drive object or object of drive gratification is appeased, and finds a channel of expression in creative work. In both giving and receiving the creative process lessens the feeling of loneliness and separation. A feeling of being united with something arises, as, for instance, in a youth walking barefoot on grass and having the sensation of being part of nature and his environment, or in the mourner expressing his sorrow in a poem. It is a state of being both alone and together with another that Winnicott has derived from the transitional phenomenon of childhood. In the later stages of development the creative experience is one of both personal uniqueness and acceptance of existing conventions. It is a region where separation anxiety is played with or worked through, where isolation and the dread of total solitude on the one hand, and unification and fusion with others on the other, prevail.

Greenacre (1957), in her conceptualization of the artist's love affair with the world, emphasizes the creative person's capacity for flexibility of attachment in object relations, as well

as his ability either to expand or intensify established relationships. According to Greenacre artistic creativity presupposes
a specific intensity of emotions and their formation. Such a
capacity in early childhood leads the artist into early relationships with both animate and inanimate objects in the environment as well as in nature. The so-called "collective alternates"
therefore lead to early personal relationships. Weissman
(1971) points out that the produced objects of an artist's
creativity, in contrast to his real objects, reflect an origin and a
conception worked through into esthetic forms and originating
from the collective alternates and transitional phenomena of
early childhood. In creatively active people the transitional
objects have been extended into collective alternates which are
the forerunners of created objects. Weissman contends that
while ordinary noncreative people live through their transi-
tional-object phase in childhood without much concern,
creatively gifted people, in contrast, hold onto collective alternates throughout their lives. Old created objects that are the
result of the creative process are subject to the same fate as
transitional objects: they lose their meaning but they are not
forgotten or repressed, nor are they mourned or internalized.

THE ESSENTIALLY FEMININE

In an artistic creation, as well as in individual creative
activity in general, two main lines can be detected. One of
them finds its expression in grandiosity, in strength, in power,
in precision, in striking effect, and so on. This approach relies
on various phallic symbols that make it possible for the creatively productive or receptive person to identify himself
either with the phallicly predominant or the phallicly submissive element, and it signifies a creative experience for those
who are in search of mastering or of submitting in phallic
devotion. An extreme example is the admiration and sensation

of creativity felt in the presence of the phallic power symbols of the ancient Egyptian pharaohs, even though their individuality is completely unknown. In phallic creative cultures femininity is conceived of as serving the phallic man or as having the role of his muse.

The other main line in creativity may be described as collective art, the art created by the people expressing their manner of working together, their festivities, and their style of decorating their homes. The creative spirit is found in confident togetherness and in the working through of common sorrows. It is well exemplified by the Swedish-speaking East Bothnic peasant culture in Finland that Edith Södergran's father came from. This culture developed without the master-serf pattern, and relies strongly on the mother of the family and the home. The kitchen is the place where the family gathers, the mother is looked on as a fellow worker, and it is she who creates an atmosphere of security in the home. This culture, in which the family gathered around the mother, has held its ground; it never penetrated the cultures of the rulers, however, and therefore those who moved away from it have usually been compelled to undergo an autoplastic change.

Erikson (1951, 1968) has established the difference between boys and girls in the manifestations of creativity in their play constructions. He observed that the boys' buildings had height and slope and contained a great deal of commotion that could be controlled or reined in, whereas the girls' constructions had a restful interior that was either open or gently enclosed, and either peaceful or open to intrusion. Erikson suggests that sexual differences bring about the polarization of styles of living, and that the procreative pattern is in varying degrees embodied in all states of excitation and inspiration, giving intensity to all experience and to its expression. The difference between the sexes is based not on the psychoanalytic concept of femininity as a modification of the so-called genital trauma of the little girl's discovering that she has no penis, but rather on the essentially feminine, meaning that woman has a specific organ for having and holding, for enclosing and protecting. This has an effect on feminine creativity. Where masculine creativity contains an opposing element to castration anxiety in the dream of a phallus of admiration, power, and honor, feminine creativity has another goal.

Greenacre (1960) states that woman's creative peculiarity is not dependent on creative potentiality in early childhood or on special neurotic characteristics, but rather on the specific anatomical structure she has for the biologically creative function of childbearing. In a woman the fantasies connected with the act of creating are more concerned with purely emotional and personal aspects, and, according to Erikson, are more related to fantasies of caring, molding, and increasing. He states, furthermore, that woman's intimacy with pain, inbred through sexual experience and motherhood, allows her to undergo pain as something meaningful without any trace of masochism. It is conceivable that her creative activity is a laborious striving to understand and relieve suffering, and to endure unavoidable pain. A woman probably has a greater capacity for mourning work because to her the pain of sorrow is not without meaning.

Greenacre (1960) thinks that woman's peculiar characteristic creativity, as already described, causes her to be less exact in externalizing, and to produce works of art in a lesser degree than men. A woman's strong illusion of having a real, hidden, invisible phallus may, according to Greenacre, give her a special talent for fulfilling her inspiration. In contrast to man's creative impulses, the productive creativity built on such a phallic illusion may easily become impossible for a woman when she is faced with inherently feminine qualities in herself, her periods of menstruation and occasional pregnancy. Greenacre presents three developmental patterns for a girl's realization of her artistic creativity:

(1) It may go into eclipse at puberty as she gives up the imaginary phallic world in favor of the more regular feminine goals and aims. (2) She regresses to the anal level, depending on the earlier vicissitudes of this period, and develops a restraining compulsiveness. (3) She abandons her feminine identification largely or almost completely in her official life, although it still teams up with the phallic identification in the bisexual activity of her artistically creative work [p. 588].

Like Erikson (1968) and Winnicott (1971), Greenacre (1960) emphasizes that productivity as such is a channel for creativity to find its outlet, but that it is not a measure of an inborn creative potential. They also point out the meaning of the bisexual identification in productive creativity. In itself it includes a receiving, keeping, and delivering element, and according to Winnicott creativity is a woman's privilege that has a masculine aspect. He refers to a female element in every human being that includes the experience of being, of being-one-with-another, and that includes the projective and the introjective identifications with the oral mother. The male element includes active doing, and this identification is based on several psychic mechanisms also in later childhood. Thus Winnicott refers to a prephallic feminine passivity and to an at least partly prephallic masculine activity.

Greenacre (1960) has found that creative people have a strong bisexual identification when in the throes of inspired creative work, and that they are likely to put aside their personal selves for the forcefully creative spirit of the artist. She also points out that many artistically talented people have several self-images with more or less differing identities, primarily those of the creative artist and the everyday common citizen.

In conclusion, it can be pointed out that creative work allows the individual to rise above the daily routine and the toilsome realities of life, while at the same time it has a special function in mourning work. Its roots are found in the primary experience of separation from the mother, and in the ability then acquired to be alone in the presence of someone else. It has its basic pattern in woman's biological function as a child-bearer, inciting inspiration, growth, and deliverance, or procreation, pregnancy, and childbirth, respectively.

Creative inspiration is fulfilled by the individual phallic masculine activity, and the product of creation continues to live in fantasy, or even to survive its maker. The idea of surviving suggests that the created product is given the role of an auxiliary ego in mourning work in the face of the final separation, that of death (Hägglund, 1973).

EDITH SÖDERGRAN'S POETRY

Edith Södergran herself defined the goal and aim of her poetry in a statement to a friend (Olsson, 1949): "I do not make poetry, I create my own being; my poems are a pathway to my self." She described her struggle to verbalize the need to create in the following passage (Olsson, 1949): "The repentant spirit has no need to seek ethical perfection in his verse, he needs only to call forth the depth of his suffering; the path may pass over stock and stone, over vanity and banality, yet he shall rise to heights where he suddenly no longer stands in uncertainty and his weakness falls off like scales." One may approach Edith Södergran's poetry with either the esthetic-lyrical aspect or the psychological aspect in mind. In her production of verse she quite obviously strove to clarify certain aspects of her own psyche. The keynote in her production seems to be a continuous mourning process, and in it she struggles to achieve understanding and clarity. She lives in the company of isolation and death and finds a meaning in them, yet she is in search of the hidden secret within herself that will solve the inconceivability of them. Her need to find a form for separation and death can be understood through her childhood experiences, when, within a short period of time in early adolescence, she lost her grandmother, her foster sister, and her father, and herself fell ill with the same disease her father had had, pulmonary tuberculosis.

In the light of her early poetry and the scraps of information her very few friends have been able to supply about her life conditions, the purpose of the mourning work in her adult verse becomes comprehensible. It puts the reader in a position to experience the various phases of the mourning process in a productive way, in the very same way that Södergran herself experienced it, in the creative spirit of a genius. The feeling of almightiness she often describes as following her depressive mourning periods can be explained as an expression of her "healthy" omnipotence; every time she passes through the phase of mourning safely, and finds herself still there after all the losses, is felt like a miracle.

Edith Södergran's Schoolgirl Poetry

There are people of literary genius, though they are very few, who, without being actually psychotic, make a strange and odd impression on the reader. Edith Södergran is such a one. In private life as well as in literary circles she is generally described as a "strange bird," and in relation to her writing it has been suggested that this impression arises from her Continental background or from the Russian-Byzantine traits in her style of writing. Descriptions of Södergran's peculiarities, as seen by others, extend from astonished neighbors' remarks on finding the odd young lady of good birth but small means carrying on a conversation with her garden flowers about the slanderously insulting column of a newspaper reporter commenting on crazy poetry, to the somewhat scented epithet of Huldra, a Scandinavian fairy queen, given to her by her devoted friend Hagar Olsson.

Her poetry clearly reveals that she made a great myth of
reality and of herself. Even in her contemplation of external
reality her gaze was directed toward her inner self. The narcissistic features in many of her poems convey the impression that
she identified herself with the devoted lover. Like a believer, at
times she approaches herself and her fragile mortal clay as if it
were an altogether too perishable temple. True enough, this
makes for a new distance from the body, but it also leaves it
vulnerable to the manifestation of the unheard-of.

In order to find an explanation for Edith Södergran's
relationship to herself and the objects that form an important
part of the background for her writing, it is essential to delin-
eate her biographical and familial dynamic circumstances.
She was born in 1892 in St. Petersburg when her parents had
been married for almost two years, and she was the only child.
Her father, Matts Södergran, was 46, a technician by trade,
born in Narpes, Finland, the oldest child of a peasant.
Tidestrom (1949) supposes that he was given an education on
account of his frailness, as a younger son was put in charge of
the farm. Matts Södergran's life had been an eventful one by
the time his daughter was born. He had spent a short time at
sea, after which he tried his hand at many trades in various
parts of Finland and Russia. This was his second marriage, his
first wife having died of tuberculosis after a four-year marriage
during which two children were born and died in infancy. His
second wife's name was Helena Holmroos; her parents came
from the Turku archipelago, and her father had been a
successful and relatively wealthy man. Helena was the only
child. She had had a love affair in her youth, having to bear
the consequences by giving birth to an illegitimate child who
died at the age of two weeks.

Her marriage to Matts Södergran must have been a bewil-
dering experience for Helena Holmroos. On the one hand, it
did provide her with a social escape from a predicament that
in those times must have been nothing short of a scandal. On

the other hand, she was the only child in a family with decidedly high social ambitions, while Matts Södergran had not, at the age of 46, been able to achieve a position of esteem in society. Helena Holmroos had often shown signs of her wish to become a fine and distinguished lady. For example, on a visit to Switzerland with her daughter she gave the impression that Edith's father had been a professor of philology at Helsinki University, and was consequently addressed as "Frau Doktor." It may be surmised, moreover, that Helena Södergran's contempt and hatred for her husband accumulated further with his failures in business involving her money, and of course with his increasing consumption of alcohol. The mother's ambitions and strong desire to be considered a well-read woman probably had an impact on the daughter's later attitudes, especially since the girl's father seemed quite indifferent to such matters. It is of course impossible to discover the extent to which the increasing destructive phallic rivalry was complemented by other more constructive influences. There is no question, however, that the marriage was an acute stroke of misfortune for both partners. For Helena Södergran the marriage, at least in part, must have been a constant reminder of the disappointment of her first intimate relationship with a man, a relationship that had been the cause of social contempt and had aroused hatred. Matts Södergran, on his part, must have felt bitter at being reminded of his failure to establish himself either socially or economically in life, having to rely not on his own means but on those of his wife, and suffering snubs on account of his lesser education and coarse manners.

The family moved back and forth between St. Petersburg and a country house in Raivola on the Karelian isthmus that had been bought with the wife's father's money. Beginning in 1902 Edith Södergran attended the German St. Petrischule in St. Petersburg, a school that was held in high esteem and had very ambitious goals. Mother and daughter lived in St. Petersburg during the school terms, while the father seems to have lived in Raivola the year round. When Edith was 12 years old, her father fell ill with what was later found to be pulmonary tuberculosis. Tidestrom (1949) has described her reaction to her father's illness as follows: "Edith is said to have been very gentle toward him during his illness, and she used to kiss him quite often. Very early her mother had her own suspicions about his illness and believed it to be more serious than was then thought. The neighbors witnessed her attempts to stop the girl from kissing her father and to keep her away from his company." Her father died when Edith was 15, and about eight months earlier she had written the first of her poems that have been found. From January, 1907, to the summer of 1909 she kept a diary, making her entries in verse form. This school-girl poetry, later called *Vaxdukshaftet* (*Exercisebook Poems*), and not published until after her death, is not to be considered a fair copy but rather as rough notes in chronological order. This, of course, adds to their value in the psychological sense, and they provide a rich array of her reactions to her father's illness and resulting death.

The winter and spring poems before the father's death show how she is searching for an object for her emotions, and how her mind is preoccupied by questions of health and illness. The poem "Through My Life" ("Durch mein Leben") has been interpreted by Enckell (1961) as echoing the terrifying experience she had when her foster sister Singa ran away from home and was later found at the railway station, dead and mutilated:

> Through my life you fled
> With hasty steps, my sweet,
> And your pretty feet
> Only the faintest mark have left.
>
> You hastened so rashly through my life,
> You could not abide by me,
> From all the misery around you
> You turned your face not to see.

It wasn't for the sake of pity
That your sweet lips curled,
You found it so repelling
That all is not sound like you.

The sight of all the misery
Made you hasten on your path,
I carry the bleeding traces
In the innermost of my heart.

Enckell assumes this poem to have been written before
Matts Södergran was admitted for treatment to Nummela
Sanatorium. Edith has projected on Singa her own feelings of
unhappiness and anxiety about her father, who was sick and
would not live long. But one cannot rule out the possibility
that she has perceived the connection correctly when, in the
verses "Fleeing You" ("Flyende du"), she sees the healthy young
person overcome by distaste for sick and depressing surroundings. This is an indication of the not so rare attitude of
the mourner toward one who has passed away, in this case
Singa, that his lot is the easier one and that he has escaped all
the painful sorrow. At the same time this state of mind makes
it easier for the adolescent poetess to carry the burden of guilt
after the sister's death and the revulsion she feels at her father's
illness.

In another poem from the same period, called "What I
Love" ("Was ich liebe"), she removes her feelings about the
ailing father to a distance by saying that long ago she had felt a
weakness for anything "unhealthy." She used to love expressions like "the heavy smell of lilacs," "gloomy glances,"
"feverish lips," and "painful smiles." She is now rid of this "bad
taste," and she loves only "healthy life" as she has found it in
the idolized person of the French teacher, M. Henri Cottier. As
in many other poems, so in this one too she tries to cut herself
free of the powerful attraction she feels for her father and to
gear her love toward the teacher who stands for the strong,
healthy father figure. Her sick father and his impending death

awaken an admixture of fear and desire in her mind. Father, the oedipal object, whom the strong teacher now represents, is the object of her libidinal interest, while his death arouses fearful premonitions of having to share his fate. She finds protection against this danger in a splitting of emotions, of which the destructive element blended with compassion is expressed in the following stanzas:

> The waves carry the moaning
> To the castle of the Russian Czar,
> Who finds no peace nor rest tonight,
> But keeps pulling his hair.

> Sweat is pouring from his brow,
> He dares not make a move,
> He would gladly bend his neck
> Under the axe on the executioner's block.

> No executioner comes to deliver him,
> The night seems never to end,
> He dares not moan, and cold sweat
> Is covering his sticky hands.

The poem seems to express quite acutely her strongly felt anxiety for the weak and tragic father, attributes equally befitting the unhappy Czar of Russia, Nicholas II. The anger partly arises from despair at witnessing the suffering of a close person and death wishes evoked by the anguish, and partly from a dreadful fear of the self being absorbed into the misery.

Enckell (1961) has described Edith Södergran's infatuation with her teacher during the winter, spring, and summer before her father's death as an awakening erotic passion, and sees a further significant connection in the teacher's short visit to Raivola during the summer, as well as in the attentions of a young man who visited the Södergran house at the same time, making the young girl strongly and alarmingly aware of his courtship. But in none of the poems of this period is there any suggestion of an erotic experience that might have had frightening implications for her. On the contrary, the two men became substitute outside objects for the oedipal love of the father that was reactivated in the crisis of adolescence. The "exercise book" indicates that in the summer of 1907 she went through a crisis related, on the one hand, to the maturing process of adolescence, and, on the other, to the mourning of her father's death. The fusion of the oedipal love object of the youthful crisis with hypercathexis of emotions of the mourning work evidently led to an eroticization of the loss. Father-lover and father-death are merged and appear frighteningly enticing to the 15-year-old girl. In a letter to the physician of the sanatorium she describes the emotions she felt during a visit to her ailing father at the age of 15: "I am horribly superstitious about Nummela. When I visited my father there during his illness I was immensely afraid, dreadfully repelled by death, overcome by the fear of this disease, this slow conscious dying" (Tidestrom, 1949, p. 76). She experienced the adolescent attraction to and panic and dread at the nearness of the oedipal object, and she associated them with death. She found refuge in her emotions for her French teacher, who stood at a proper distance both as a person and because of his manner of speech, for he spoke German with a foreign accent that she found very amusing.

At the end of May, 1907, Matts Södergran was discharged from Nummela without hope of recovery. A day after her father's homecoming Edith wrote the poem "Our Home" ("Unser Haus") in her "exercise book." The poem begins with an endearing description of the Raivola home, but the last stanza shatters the illusion, and she is very critical of herself for being dishonest and banal. In the poem "Life" ("Das Leben"), written during two following days, she says:

Life is earnest and sad and clear,
Therefore every sensation is true.

Pretense of love and pretense of pain,
Never take the seeker far.

It is quite conceivable that these poems are a prelude to a depressive period that lasted until June of the same year. The few poems produced during this period bear the marks of low spirits and sadness. The eyes of the ill father fascinate and stun the girl, and she mourns his misery (e.g., in the poem "Where" ["Wozu"]).

In the middle of June a sudden change takes place. In a poem of June 17 she says she can hear near by the whizzing sound of a scythe, but her heart is singing for joy. Enckell (1961) has emphasized that "After this period one looks in vain for even the slightest mention of her father in her poetic diary; only a few of the summer poems echo the low spirits that reflect the depressive mood prevailing in the home." Tidestrom (1949) has tried to find an explanation for her feelings toward her father in that "they were so conflicting that she could not give expression to them in poetic form." This was about four months before her father's death, and it is obvious that at that time she tried to flee from reality and sorrow. In view of the fact that her later poetry does not include any aggressive elements, it may be surmised that in her mourning crisis she evaded the aggressiveness of sorrow that would have been directed at her father. He had failed to fulfill her childhood expectations by falling ill and dying, and her earlier experiences, together with the hard realities of life, made it impossible for her to work through the most stinging disappointment and the pain of sorrow. In the abrupt exclusion of mourning work in her youth may be found the reason for her attraction to and idolatry of elderly men and philosophers, and ultimately even death as the greatest authority.

In a poem called "K......" written in mid-July, she intimates that there is something that is taboo and cannot be confided to a soul. The poem is supposedly written to a friend,

Klaudia, who had visited her that summer. According to Tidestrom (1949), "the most intimate and the most atrocious" in the poem that she could not disclose even to her best friend is an indication of the "frightening" erotic experience that was also the cause of the jubilant outburst in another poem, written on June 17. Enckell (1961) supposes that the poem "belongs to the gloomy shadow that, with the ill father's presence, had fallen upon the Raivola home," and that the poetess "carried the secret wish for her father's death" in her heart. The poem seems to indicate that she had ruled out the possibility of telling her friend about her sorrow. This suggests the universally conceived taboo concerning erotic emotions toward the oedipal object and death wishes toward one who is the cause of sorrow and pain. Of course, both oedipal love and death wishes are quite unconscious in adolescence, whereas in the poem they are subject to consideration at a conscious level. The poem indicates that she has come to realize that the deepest sorrow, the truest misery, is not to be disclosed to one's friends. This attitude is associated with the emotional distance that is usually taken from a deeply mourning person. Only a beloved person can share deep sorrow, and only an adult can go through the experience of mutual mourning with the dying person. Mutually experienced sorrow intensifies the atmosphere of intimacy and the sensation of togetherness surrounding the deathbed. For Södergran in her adolescence this was not possible. Separation from parents in adolescence usually takes place gradually, in favorable circumstances, through growing independence and freedom from emotional bondage. In contrast, the separation through death is a sudden one, and the adolescent withdraws to a distance from the dying parent, driven by the anxiety evoked by oedipal intimacy. At an early age Södergran discovered that she could not share her sorrow with anyone, nor could she, later on in life, become sufficiently intimate with another person. She preferred to work through the mourning process alone in her poetry, by means of her own creativity. Her poetry should not, therefore, be interpreted as autistic writing, but be seen as pointing distinctly in a certain direction at a certain goal. It gives her the necessary intimacy to continue in the mourning work. This is a manifestation of Winnicott's transitional phenomenon — to be alone in the presence of someone else — the starting point for all creativity to be later introjected as a personal ability. Södergran substituted creative genius and fantasy objects for the real heterosexual relationships she could not form.

At the time of her father's death she gave expression to her hunger for love and the pain that seems to have been without an object and therefore expanded into a *Weltschmerz*. In the poem of March 13 she says she is without a homeland in the world, and that no friendly savior will show her the way to the secret land whose existence she senses like a strange tune following her everywhere, yet never caught:

Without a homeland I am in this world,
My homeland is a spellbound land,
No road leads there, there is no pain
There is no love, nor kind savior.

All through life a tune is heard
That forebodings, dreams, and losses
Are our lot. This tune keeps ringing
Day and night and never leaves my ears.

The tune keeps following me for always
But my tongue cannot give it expression,
And in some chance human countenance
I suddenly see the tune come to life.

And I want to grasp it and to understand
But gone is the shimmering shadow;
With pain in my heart I must go onward,
And I keep looking on and on, yet never find.

The heavy depression she suffered from, at least periodically, during the spring after her father's death found expression in her death fantasies. In the poem of March 6 dreams of love and death are interwoven. She describes how, deep at the bottom of the sea, shivering and bound by the seaweed, she is taken into the arms of her loved one:

My beloved comes and into his arms
He tenderly takes me at midnight,
I tremble in his sweet embrace
From the very bottom of my heart.

We are both shivering with fever
We are cold and feel not well
And we love the painful reflection
Of the sun at the bottom of the sea.

In another poem, of May 7, she devotes herself to an elaboration of her own autopsy. She pictures herself dead from anguish without ever having donned the adult woman's corselet or ever bearing a child. She is cut in two, her lungs are exposed and found to be black, like bloodstained dust, and it is established that it all started from the lungs. It is found that her abnormal heart and chaotic mind were the cause of death. A strong identification with the tubercular and dead father is manifested while at the same time she is subjected to massive physical assault. Identification with, and perhaps incorporation of, the lost object in the mourning work has taken this form. The sad feeling of emptiness has not led to activity by way of identification, but rather to a fantasy of being empty, unimpregnated, and of becoming pregnant by the father's death, of contracting the same pulmonary disease he had. The emptiness of sorrow has been united with the fantasy of the emptiness of the woman's inner space. She gives expression to the unconscious wish to be pregnant, to fill the inner space with the father, with his illness and his death. She actually

contracts tuberculosis later on, and in the psychic sense it can
be said that she fills the inner space in her poetry as an adult
woman with fantasies, ideas, and emotions of the oedipal
object and the reunion with the object.

In the autumn of 1908 Edith Södergran fell ill, and by the
turn of the year her illness was identified as pulmonary tuberculosis. According to Tidestrom, she wrote her first free verse
at about the same time. We shall compare one of her "school-
girl poems" from the time right after her father's death with
the poem Tidestrom considers to be the first of the "truly
Södergranic" poems. The first one reads as follows:

> A frightened bird is flying
> And moaning in the sky
> One can see the gray of the feathers
> So clearly in the white of the snow.
>
> The poor gray bird
> Has lost itself in the snow,
> And I'm overcome by a thought
> I'm overcome and I'm stunned.
>
> I want to fly like the bird
> Until I can find the path
> Through whirling snow and through fog,
> In the cold raw wind.

And the other one:

> Joy is a butterfly
> That flutters low over the ground,
> But sorrow is a bird
> With big, strong, black wings
> That carry one high over life,
>
> That floats down into the sunshine and foliage.
> The bird of sorrow rises high,
> Where the angels of pain keep watch
> Over the beds of death.

It is apparent that the bird here is a father and death symbol. In the earlier poem, written before her father's death, the bird is a weak, confused, and pitiful thing that arouses compassion and also vague anxiety about identifying with father. The very fact that the young poetess contracted the same disease her father had is an indication that the dark bird has joined her, and together they form an imposing and fruitful yet dreadful mythical entity.

POETRY OF THE MATURE POETESS

"The Joyous Year"

From the time after sanatorium treatment, first at Nummela, later in Davos, Switzerland; there are poems of Södergran to be found from the spring of 1913 onward. The time period closely following she called "The Joyous Year" ("Det glada aret"), when she was back at home after a long, dreary partnership with her disease and the danger of impending death. Following this period her debut collection, called *Poems,* was written and published in 1916.

Poems expresses joy and recklessness at having conquered the danger the disease meant to her. Thoughts of death are a constantly present theme, and she describes how she wins death by her powerful love, "how she looks upon old times with new eyes" in the poem "The Old House" ("Det gamla huset"), how she "longs for her old graves" but "must wait for the gentle death." She speaks slightingly of man and denies his power of attraction for her in the poem "Violet Twilight" ("Violetta skymningar"):

Man has not come, has never been,
shall never be . . .
Man is a false mirror the daughter of the sun
in rage throws against the cliff,
man is a lie the white child does not grasp,
man is a rotten fruit proud lips despise.

Instead she has eroticized suffering, sadness, and death. In the poem "For All Four Winds" ("Mot alla fyra vindar") she says:

> I have a gate for all four winds,
> I have a golden gate for the east—for
> love that will never come,
> I have a gate for the day, and another for
> gloom,
> I have a gate for death—that is always open.

She describes being with child by death in the poem "We Women" ("Vi kvinnor"):

> He came one cold day with empty eyes,
> He went away on a heavy day with lost memories on his
>   brow.
> If my child does not live, it is his.

In the poem "Last Flower of Autumn" ("Hostens sista blomma") she pictures herself as the last one to survive, and says that "as the last one it is so easy to die," and "I shall shut the gates of death." Because of the intense eroticization of death she obviously understands that she has overcome the deadly danger, made friends with the enemy, and by reaction formation and denial of fear she is able to maintain the idea that her life continues and that pain will release her and give her new hope of life. Even hell is wonderful, and she describes it with some irony as a "happy" intrauterine existence in the poem "Hell" ("Helvetet"):

> Oh how magnificent is not hell!
> In hell nobody speaks of death.
> Hell is built in the bowels of the earth
> and adorned with glowing flowers . . .
> In hell no one says an empty word . . .
> In hell no one has drunk and no one has slept
> and no one rests and no one sits still.

In hell no one talks, but all scream,
Tears there are not tears and all sorrow is powerless.
In hell no one becomes ill and no one tires.
Hell is never-changing and everlasting.

While writing her first volume, *Poems,* she also wrote the first poems of *The Land That Is Not* (*Landet som icke är*). This series of poems, which she wrote alongside of her other poetic work, was intended to be kept in her desk drawer, and it was not published until after her death. It obviously deals with a conscious splitting of emotions. Where the world is allowed to admire her positive emotions in *Poems,* the contents of the collection *The Land That Is Not* are sorrow, disillusionment, and consciousness of approaching death. In the poem "To Eros" ("Till Eros") she says:

Eros, you cruelest of gods,
why took you me to this dark land?

. . . .

I do not flee, I do not wait,
I only suffer like an animal.

In the poem "Nothing" ("Ingenting") she tries, in a realistically gloomy way, to calm her fear of death by hoping that after all there is something far away and that she is not living in vain, while she defends herself against the temptations her death fantasies represent for her:

Be calm, my child, there is nothing,
and all is as you see it: the woods, the smoke and the flash
    of lights.
Somewhere far away in a far-off land
the sky is more blue, stone walls are covered with roses,
or there is a palm tree and a sweeter wind —
and that is all.
No more than snow is on the branches of the spruce,

Nothing is there to kiss with warm lips,
and all lips, in time, become cool.
But you say, my child, that your heart is strong,
and to live in vain is less than to die.
What would you unto death? Can you feel the repulsion his
    clothes are spreading
and nothing is more sickening than taking one's own life.
We should love life's long hours of illness
and the crowded years of waiting,
as we do the short moments when the desert is in bloom.

The Land That Is Not can be considered a continuation of the verse diary of her youth, which served for working through her sorrow after her father's death. In this volume she is working through her own dying process, which to her is purely personal and private. It may therefore be considered highly narcissistic, because beside the primary narcissism directed at one's own self and bodily functions, there is also the secondary narcissism that during the dying process is directed at the person herself. In this "diary" of "the land that is not" she comes very close to the inconceivable, to the state of not being, in an earnest way without evoking unbearable anxiety or impressions of banality, sensations that are easily created by thinking of death as a defense against anxiety.

The Saint George Period

The volumes *September Lyre* (*Septemberlyran*), *Rose Altar* (*Rosenaltare*), and *Shadow of the Future* (*Framtidens skugga*) that now followed were written during the four years from 1916 to 1920. In these poems we can see how Sodergran, like Saint George, represses her fear and powerlessness in the face of impending death. She fights the dragon, the menacing death, and fancies herself to be in possession of the prophetic powers of a saint. "She dreams of giving birth to the whole world and of elevating life to a higher plane with the aid of chosen obedient spirits who are silently working to free mankind" (Olsson, 1949). She writes about herself: "My self-confidence is due to the discovery of my dimensions. It does not befit me to make myself smaller than I am" (Prologue to *September Lyre*). In the poem "Triumph in Being" ("Triumf at finnas till") she expresses the feeling of mightiness, and death is given a feminine form:

> What do I fear? I am part of eternity.
> I am part of the great power of all things,
> a lonely world among a million worlds,
> a star of first degree that goes out last.
>
> . . . .
> Time — convertress, time — mutilatress,
> Time — enchantress,
> do you come with new intrigues, a thousand guiles
> to offer me an existence
> like a tiny seed, like a coiling snake, like
> a rock in the sea?
> Time — you murderess — begone!

With phallic power she wants to master time, the woman, and with cunning to fool death, the old man, in the poem "Little Old Man" ("Lillgubben"):

> The little old man is sitting and counting eggs,
> Each time he counts, one egg is missing.
> Show him not your gold, my friends.

With an even greater phallic power of her own she defies and castrates the phallic symbols and the danger in the poem "The Bull" ("Tjuren"):

> What is keeping the bull?
> My nature is a red cloth.
> Do I not see bloodshot eyes,
> do I not hear the short, panting breath,

does not the ground tremble under the rage of hooves?
No.
The bull has no horns;
he stands by the manger
and chews stubbornly on his tough hay.
Unpunished the reddest cloth flutters in the wind.

The Saint George period in Södergran's poetry can be
looked on as an attempt, by means of a phallic illusion, to gain
greater influence in becoming the chosen one, to overcome the
fear of nothingness and the fear of falling into oblivion as
worthless. She now wants to castrate the death that she had
wanted to charm in her erotic verse during "the joyous year."
She transforms death into a woman, into an old man, into an
inanimate hornless bull, and into something that cannot reach
her. Especially during this time she becomes attracted to the
ideas of philosophers like Schopenhauer and Nietzsche and the
anthroposophist Rudolf Steiner. She believes she derives her
magic phallic powers from the gods, and by using this power
she thwarts the phallic threat of death, the reaper. Like a
rejected woman who has unsuccessfully tried to seduce her
lover, death, erotically, she now turns to other powerful men,
philosophers and gods, from whom she gets the phallic power
to castrate the traitor, death. When she finds that her woman's
means have been ineffective in warding off the danger, death,
by eroticization, she resorts to a phallic defense. These fancies
of her imagination are well expressed in the poem "The World
Was Reduced to a Heap of Ashes" ("Jorden blev forvandlad till
en askhog"):

The world was reduced to a heap of ashes.
Dressed in the vest of a repentant
I gently sit upon it and dream.
Oh, how blest are my dreams!
I am strong,
for I have arisen from death's marble bed.

Death — I looked upon your face, I held the scales for you.
Death — your embrace is not cold, I myself am the flame.
Who is God? What has he done to us?
Do not blaspheme! He is near.

. . . .

Over the earth from a silver cup I throw passion,
besides which Aphrodite's dreams grow pale.

Södergran's struggle to overcome her anxiety about her
weakness in the face of death by seeking help from the
devotion of philosophers and gods can be conceived of as a
repetition of her fleeing from sorrow and helplessness at the
time of her father's death in her youth. She had then consciously belittled her father and his distress, and had turned
her devotion to other elderly authorities. She uses the same
defense mechanism against the sorrow of loss of herself when
death is threatening.

With illusory phallic strength she fights for the improvement of humanity and for its continued existence. In her poems
she summons people to follow her; in the poem "Mystery"
("Mysteriet") she even calls on them to receive the ointment for
the future from her hands, and declares that her sword shall
not rest "until the earth is a garden where gods dream at the
brims of wonderful cups." She feels that humanity is in
danger, under a threat, and with the mightiness of gods, as in
the poem "Creators" ("Skapargestalter"), she transforms "the
great mass of men into a joy for gods." She externalizes her
own impending destruction, and by way of reaction formation
she mourns over the welfare of humanity instead of hoping for
help in her hour of need. At the same time she protects
humanity against her own aggressions that arise from the
sorrow of losing her fellow men. Here we meet again the same
pattern of reacting that was seen in the loss of her father, when
she suppressed the aggressive emotions of sorrow by means of
idealization.

By the end of this period the phallic illusion recedes, and doubt rises to the surface. She questions truth in the poem "Hamlet":

Truth, truth, do you live in the mortuary among
worms and dust?

Truth, do you live where all that I hate is found?
Truth, do woeful lanterns light your path?

At the end of the Saint George period, from 1919 to 1920, Södergran wrote a few poems in sequence with *The Land That Is Not*. In these poems she expresses her imprisonment, her isolation, and her inability fully to grasp great ideas. To herself she expresses the opposite of what she gives to the world in her published verse. In "Palehearted Night" ("Blekhjartade natt") she writes:

An abandoned castle rules the world,
the nameless castle of power.

And in the poem "My Life, My Death, and My Fate" ("Mitt liv, min dod och mitt ode") she says:

All is dark around me,
I cannot lift a straw.
I have but one desire, but I know it not.
When it bursts forth, I shall die:
Hail thee, my life, my death and my fate.

The Last Three Years

During the last three years before her death at midsummer in 1923, Södergran produced very little. She died at the age of 31, and we are given a glimpse into her last years in her letters to Olsson (1955). In 1921 she was greatly fascinated by religious questions. First she turned her back on Schopenhauer and on Nietzsche's ideas of *Ubermensch*. She writes on January 30: "... I found it difficult to wrench myself free of him

[Nietzsche]. Sometimes I weep for longing for the *Ubermensch;* it is a purely physical feeling, the fancy of a pregnant woman"; and on March 16: "I have abandoned the *Ubermensch;* I look upon him as my double." She turned to Steiner and his teachings of reincarnation, and found a fellow anthroposophist in Raivola. She soon gave up Steiner, however, partly influenced by Olsson, who did not take him seriously. She then turned to the Gospels, and found in Olsson the most important object of her deepest emotions. She wrote to Olsson on August 29: "I don't understand the holy ghost, but I think you are not wriggling in the net as Steiner would have the world wriggling with him. I believe that you know something about Christ that no one else knows, something even the apostles did not really understand." During 1921 it seems that she had lost her belief in conquering the world with phallic power and bringing about the salvation of mankind by surrendering to reformers of humanity.

In her last three years she turned to nature, and tried to make contact with Olsson and some other poets. She worked very hard to finish an anthology of poems. The anthology was an auxiliary ego meant to outlive her, and she withstood a great deal for this work. She demanded much time from Olsson, who sometimes was at a loss to find it for her. On her deathbed she wrote her last greeting to Olsson: "Has she forgotten me, Hagar, are we not bound together in life and death? A fountain of devotion springs up in my innermost, in my hour of purity I call upon you, my Lord of my heart's child, in the sweetest of the pure moments I remember Hagar." Olsson was the object of her positive emotions, and she lived their friendship through once more in death.

In September, 1922, she notes in "Thoughts of Nature" ("Tankar om naturen"): "The religious secrets are secrets of nature." Her last poems are variations on this theme, and she searched intensely for intimacy with nature around her home.

In her last poems from the volume *The Land That Is Not*

one finds regression to childhood religious beliefs and to mother nature. In the poem "The Tree of My Childhood" ("Mitt barndoms träd") she says: "... the key to all secrets is hidden in the grass on the raspberry hill ...," and in "Oh Heavenly Clarity" ("O himmelska klarhet"):

> And the halo shining on the brow of a saint
> is not as clear and great,
> as the crown on the head of a human child
> in his tender years.
> And earth and flowers and stones they speak
> their language to the child,
> and the child he answers and crows in reply
> in the language of creation.

In the poem "Home-Coming" ("Hemkomst") she describes how she relinquishes everything else and desires only union with nature. In another poem without a name, beginning with the words "There is not a soul in the world who has time," the dying person's splitting of emotions is displayed, the ambivalence dividing into the bad—the earthly—and the good—the unknown that comes after death:

> But a little worm saw in the dark dream
> that moonlight split his being in two:
> one was nothing,
> the other was all things and God himself.

The poems *The Land That Is Not* and "Arrival in Hades" ("Ankomst till Hades") were found by Södergran's mother after her death. In them she describes how death silences everything and the dying asks questions that have only one answer: "I am the one that you love and shall always love." Here she puts into words the last narcissistic love of a dying person. As a sign of well-advanced mourning work in relinquishing both life and the fantasies of the kingdom of death, the following lines may be quoted:

My life was a hot delusion,
But one thing I have found, and one thing
I have certainly won, —
The way to the land that is not.

DISCUSSION

From the psychoanalytic point of view the description of
the mourning work Edith Södergran gives in some detail in her
poetry and notes is of great interest and importance, because
the process is worked through with the aid of creative talent
instead of psychotherapeutic support from another person,
with the regression and the transference to the therapist that
follow. For the young poetess creative work has replaced
human relationships and provided her with the sensation of
being part of the world that she needed. She was not psychotic or autistic, nor was she struggling to gain control over or
to possess other people by means of imagined power.

Because of her creative talent she was in possession of a
a highly developed capacity for working through the mourning
process. The characteristic phases of the dying process are
plainly displayed in her work: first, in the denial of threatening
death by means of conquering it with her own strength;
second, in relinquishing the cathected object, including her
own body, after having worked through the hypercathexis and
the culmination of aggressions in sorrow. Similarly, we find the
formation of an auxiliary ego, a splitting of the ambivalent
emotions, and finally the fusion with the primary object, the
mother (see Chapter 1).

Södergran's poetry reflects the four different phases of her
development, phases that all have dominating mechanisms of
their own in the defense against the threat of death and
separation anxiety. The various phases all have their unique,
characteristic creative qualities.

The schoolgirl poetry has its origin in the incapacity of the

adolescent poetess to mourn the loss of some of her very near
relatives: her maternal grandmother, her foster sister, and,
most important of all, her father. The strong need to find an
explanation for and to understand separation and death that
she had found so meaningful is evidenced in the poems of this
period. She was not freed from bondage to him after a fully
accomplished mourning work; instead, a strong father
cathexis lingered in her unconscious fantasy. One finds a split
father image in the strong phallic father that she projected
onto her teacher and later onto philosophers and reformers of
mankind. The failings of the father's character—a result of
split emotions—are found in the weak and ill father whom the
mother despises, and whom Södergran so definitely eroticized
in her poetry.

In these erotic fantasies she experienced both fear and
fascination, and father-lover and father-death became one.
She felt a strong unity with the love object that she introjected
at the same time that she fell ill with the same disease her
father had had, pulmonary tuberculosis. Afterward she felt
that the disease meant being impregnated by the father and
being with child by father-death. She was then a young woman
with an "inner space," as Erikson (1968) puts it. This inner
space she filled with fantasies of the ill father and the eroticized oedipal object, enriching and developing them with her
thoughts, her fantasies, and her emotions, finally giving them
expression in verse form. Her creative potential enables her to
express unification in contrast to loneliness, and to find
alleviation for suffering the unavoidable pain of separation.

"The joyous year" followed as a massive denial of the threat
and proximity of death after Södergran had fallen seriously ill
with tuberculosis. This phase was preceded by a period of
silence in her creative work, and should be considered the
prologue to a totally new experience. Eroticization and introjection of the father after his death had abolished the separation anxiety. When she fell ill she came face to face with death

herself. Death now became a threat to her own existence and her creative gift. When her father died she had introjected the weak, ill, and powerless father, but now she had to face menacing death as the powerful phallic threat appearing in the guise of an indomitable adversary.

During "the joyous year" she disparaged the attraction of the phallic man for her. She denied the danger of death and believed that by the strength of her love she still could eroticize hard, frightening death and make it kind and soft by her womanly means.

On a different plane from that of the mature woman, in the poems of *The Land That Is Not* a child was speaking of fear and bewilderment in the face of separation and death. In these poems she expressed her desire to find a safer land by regressing to the preoedipal phase of childhood.

When in the next phase of the dying process, the Saint George period, Södergran struggled to overcome the phallic threatening death by an even greater phallic power, she castrated death and transformed it into a feminine image. In defense of herself she identified with the aggressor, making herself the leader and spokesman for the welfare of mankind. She searched for leadership among people, and announced that she was in the possession of godly, phallic power to bring about the happiness of humanity. In this way she was striving in her fantasy to strengthen her narcissistic worth by directing the loving emotions of people to herself. Thus it would be impossible for the castrator — as she at this stage imagined death — to reach her.

During the last three years, as her defenses gradually weakened, in her attempt at first as a woman by enclosing and enriching and then by phallicly conquering the man — death — a regression to the prephallic fantasies and sensations of child-hood took place. She described the small child's security in the symbiotic intimacy with mother nature after a splitting of emotions had taken place by ascribing the bad part of her ambivalent emotions to the earthly, and the good part to the unknown, which to her had a narcissistic import in death. Finally her creative gift was allowed to engulf her own narcissistic worth, and it became an auxiliary ego that would live after her death. Here is an explanation for the absence in her poems of fantasies of life after death, which had lost its significance for her because her narcissistic libido was bound up and manifested itself in her creative production.

Södergran had a special regressive capacity to serve her ego when she wrote her poems; this capacity persisted even during a period of denying threatening death. The creative regression sought a prephallic stage while the defensive part of her poetry sprang from events experienced in the oedipal stage. Her creative experiences are characterized by traits of the transitional phenomenon, whereas the defensive elements in her production are fantasies of conquering and mastering.

PART II

A Psychoanalytic Study of
Narcissism, Phallic Defense, and Creativity
in Mourning

3.

Mourning and Narcissism

In "Mourning and Melancholia," Freud (1917) introduced the basic conceptions for the psychoanalytic understanding of grief. He says: "Mourning is regularly the reaction to the loss of a loved person, or to the loss of some abstraction which has taken the place of one, such as one's country, liberty, an ideal, and so on. . . . We rely on its being overcome after a certain lapse of time, and we look upon any interference with it as useless or even harmful" (pp. 243-244). Accordingly, the loss of an abstraction stirs up the same reactions as the loss of an inner object.

MOURNING IN RELATION TO ADAPTATION AND GROWTH

The individual ego develops in interaction with the environment from the personal experiences and events of childhood. As Freud (1923, p. 29) formulated the idea, "the character of the ego is a precipitate of abandoned object-cathexes," each essential frustration and abandonment being followed by sorrow. In this wider aspect, the mourning process becomes an important and universal means of reaction to adaptation and growth that always includes the loss of something old, while a new structure is built. Mourning invariably follows loss of libidinal cathexis, and as a result of the mourning process, the ego and superego functions are developed. In "Totem and Taboo" Freud (1913) says that mourning is attached to the positive emotions aroused by the lost object, and that, on the other hand, the satisfaction derived from the loss is connected with the triumphant emotions elicited by the aggressions—most often repressed—toward the lost object. As a result of the repression, the unconscious aggressive impulses toward the lost object become the source of pain and fear.

Freud (1917) described the mourning work that begins after the immediate reaction of grief following object loss as follows: "Reality-testing has shown that the loved object no longer exists, and it proceeds to demand that all libido shall be withdrawn from its attachments to that object" (p. 244). The continuous reality testing Freud lays so much stress on is a central element in mourning work, leading to reparative and healthy adaptation to new and changed circumstances. A precondition, however, is that the subject's ego be able to endure the immediate reactions of grief that follow object loss preceding the mourning work. It is well known that there are contradictory conceptions of the developmental stage at which the child's ego has the capacity to cope with mourning (Hägglund, 1973). According to Anna Freud (1965), mourning is possible when the child has attained the stage of object constancy, "which enables a positive inner image of the object to be maintained, irrespective of either satisfactions or dissatisfactions" (p. 65). It is then that the gradual, painful process of the libido's withdrawal from the object becomes possible.

INNER AND OUTER OBJECTS IN MOURNING

In order to endure the immediate reactions to object loss, such as the intense psychic pain of grief, the attachment to the object, and the aggressive feelings due to frustration, a good inner object and often even a good contemporary external object are required. In the course of mourning work, children are in greater need than adults of the support that a good, permanent, external object can give them in the form of an auxiliary ego (Furman, 1964a; A. Freud, 1967). Nagera (1970) lays great emphasis on the role of a secure, familiar environment as a good external object in a child's mourning work. Obviously, an adult's mourning also proceeds more profitably with good external objects.

A good outcome of the mourning process depends not only on good inner objects that supply the primary capacity for mourning, but also on external objects that alleviate separation anxiety, and, furthermore, on the creative ability developed on the basis of the transitional object conceived by Winnicott (1953). The meaning of creativity gains more importance in the light of separation anxiety, decathexis of the object and identification with it, and total integration, as external objects lose their significance (see Chapter 2).

From this point of view, mourning work means using inner objects, above all the primary object, the mother or mother substitute, who makes possible the transitional creativity for the child, and the internalization of whom and identification with whom in the mother-child relationship are the nuclei of primary narcissism. The transitional object and the experiences of the transitional phase, too, are founded on oral erotism in the relationship with the mother, and the creative ability attained during this phase includes the ability to use inanimate objects in a creative, preserving way that reinforces narcissism. It is at this point that, later in life, mourning work and creativity are fused into one experience. Creativity and the created object are cathected at the same time that libido is being withdrawn from the lost object. The hyper-cathected love object is internalized later, and identification with it takes place, bringing about reinforcement of primary narcissism or reinforcement of narcissism in the form of secondary narcissism.

THE MOURNING OF
NARCISSISTIC PERSONALITIES

It is well known that the narcissistic personality has poor object relations and is excessively self-absorbed. Kohut (1971) says that narcissistic personalities are "fixated on archaic grandiose self-configurations and/or archaic, overestimated, narcissistically cathected objects" (p. 3). Kernberg (1974) emphasizes that the primary object of a narcissistic person has been an unempathic, narcissistic, cold, and overprotective mother for whom the child's "specialness" in the mother's narcissistic world has overshadowed the child's own narcissistic value. In the mother's narcissistic world the child's grandiose fantasies of both mother and child have centered on this feeling of extraordinariness. The defensively emphasized narcissism protects the child against his narcissisic rage and against his feeling of worthlessness. He has no trust in the world, which he feels is depriving him of love; he himself is like a "hungry wolf." The narcissistic personality has internalized the primary object that frustrates him and toward whom he harbors strongly aggressive feelings. For this reason, the narcissistic personality does not react to his losses later in life with grief and mourning. The realization of grief requires, as a precondition, a good and protective inner primary object that can be trusted. The reaction of a strongly narcissistic personality to the loss of a significant object is anxiety at having been abandoned, and shame and humiliation that must be concealed. At the grave of a relative, for instance, he does not cry, but calmly controls himself and is well-behaved, unaffected, and poised.

Kernberg (1974) believes that if the person whose narcissism has been seriously traumatized in the oral phase of development aims "oral rage" and "oral envy" toward the annihilation of the primary importance of love and drive gratification, he must seek defense against childhood frustrations in withdrawal to grandiose fantasies of himself and his own uniqueness. Thus the grandiose fantasies of adulthood correspond to the childhood fantasies of the idealized parent, as well as the grandiose self. The idealized parent, the mother, has frustrated the child by her indifference to his personal needs, while praising his part in maintaining her own narcissism and in their mutually shared narcissism. The child has sensed that he has been deprived of his own narcissistic gratification, and has then converted the rage and envy aroused by the one who has deprived him, and on whom he is entirely dependent, into idealization of her and their mutual relationship. For instance, a person narcissistically traumatized in childhood may, when frustrated as an adult, retreat to "prince and princess" fantasies of rising above ordinary people out of the fear of being "immersed in the masses," which is his conception of mutual relationships between people. On the one hand, he despises the everyday contacts between "laymen"; on the other hand, he is envious of the very same thing. Similarly, the problematic structure of isolation and envy is reflected in the reactions of a narcissistic personality to the expression of frank and mutually felt grief and the ensuing creativity.

An example is the case of an adult male from a family of state officials of good social standing, who in his political career had always upheld the principle of equality, but who totally lacked the capacity for feeling empathy or for establishing intimate relationships. Only after an analysis of long duration did he disclose having felt, for the first time, compassion and pity after hearing about a shocking event. Whenever he felt frustrated he would withdraw to grandiose or sadistic-phallic fantasies. With the sudden realization of his own emotional void and of his envy of other people who could feel strongly, as well as of his tendency to control his own feelings and the wish to control those of people "reveling in their emotions," by means of his highly sophisticated intellect he developed a fantasy of suicide. As a transference experience he believed that suicide could be the solution of a situation that, for him, seemed to have come to a dead end. "By his death he would have his revenge on me for not loving him, and after losing him I would be grief-stricken and would come to realize his true worth. He would then be free of my recurrent demands 'to do nothing but associate all the time,' and he could keep his own thoughts to himself." Yet he imagined that he would be present to take note of my reactions of grief after losing him, and he felt that we would then enter into a great intimacy and unity. — The transference had its roots in his experiences with his mother. His mother's object relations had been deeply traumatized, and she had, therefore, been bent on urging the boy, by appealing to phallic-narcissistic fantasies, to do his utmost to succeed, and by his excellence to compensate for her childhood losses and suffering. Whenever the boy chanced to give expression to his sadness or his weakness, he met rejection and isolation. He hated his mother, whom he emotionally regarded as the exploiter of his narcissism, but because he was unable to mourn alone as a child when, for instance, he went to the hospital, he was entirely dependent on the mutual grandiose fantasies in order to preserve his narcissistic equilibrium. Expressing grief and working through the various phases of mourning during analysis were entirely new experiences to him, making him fear punishment by rejection or humiliation.

PHALLIC-NARCISSISTIC GRANDIOSE FANTASIES IN MOURNING

Where the oral and anal stages give rise to the development of healthy narcissism with the capacity for mourning and creativity, phallic-exhibitionistic narcissism is the token of the ego's defense against sorrow, against regressive coexistence, and against the mother envy of earlier developmental stages with the search for the extraordinary, the passion for rivalry and winning—"The ideal state of self" (a term coined by Joffe and Sandler [1965]) is, according to Mahler (1968), the climax of the child's symbiotic phase, and is representative of the complex symbiotic dual unity between child and mother. The child has then integrated the primary object, has identified with it in the form of primary narcissism, and has acquired the emotions of caring for and loving the anal object of the anal stage, which is one of the precursors of caretaking and love at the genital level, and which later in life constitutes the sublimated wish to care for and to organize, as well as the need for order, cleanliness, and regularity.

When the child has acquired object constancy at the beginning of or during the oedipal phase, he is already in possession of the capacity to mourn because of the introjected primary object. But a truly good capacity for mourning requires the support and presence of an external object. In favorable circumstances the child's small and large sorrows can be met in an atmosphere of intimacy that uses his own capacity, developed in the symbiotic phase, for temporary regression as a kind of "regression in the service of the ego." The child is then able to gain the confidence that sorrow can be shared with someone else, that it can be passed on to another, and that it joins people together. In adulthood, the same end is achieved by relying on inner objects.

If, on the other hand, the child is forbidden the regression to a symbiotic experience when losses come his way, and is instead urged to lean on phallic-omnipotent fantasies of competing and winning, of repressing and governing, that make it possible for him to bypass sorrow after loss, then he resorts to the narcissistic support of the magic-omnipotent fantasies of the symbiotic phase, and combines them with the later phallic-oedipal fantasies in which he is the victor. In this way mourning is not allowed to continue long enough, and the child, or later the adult, who suffers loss does not take refuge in symbiotic regression, but, rather, turns to the phallic fantasy in which grief is overlaid by means of an illusion of a magic-omnipotent phallus of power.

NARCISSISM IN THE VARIOUS STAGES
OF THE MOURNING PROCESS

Pollock (1961) distinguishes four stages of the mourning process in the following order: (1) the *shock* caused by the loss; (2) the emotion of *grief* as a reaction to the loss; (3) the reaction to *separation;* and (4) the reparative *adaptation* to changed circumstances. Of these, the last one corresponds to the mourning work described by Freud (1917). When one loses an important object, as is the case in the death of a close relative, the *shock* reaction upsets the equilibrium attained by the ego because the "here and now" object no longer exists. The emotional coexistence with the object is disrupted, and this realization releases a flood of emotions that at first cannot be integrated, but instead are the cause of strong verbal and physical reactions with ensuing dramatic gestures and exclamations, and finally even panic. Shock is based on the narcissistic humiliation that overcomes the subject who is unable to prevent the loss of a significant object. Eidelberg (1959) contends that "there is a sudden loss of control over external or internal reality, or both, by virtue of which the emotion of terror is produced, along with the damming up of narcissistic libido or destrudo" (p. 166). According to Pollock (1961), "the shock phase results when the ego is narcissistically immobilized by the suddenness and massiveness of the task that confronts it" (p. 346).

In the second phase of mourning, emotions of *grief* overcome the mind. At first, emotions are manifested in various muscular activities, such as restless motion, wringing the hands, touching various objects, and so on, and in weeping and grimacing to ease painful sorrow. This is reminiscent of a small child's experiencing separation anxiety according to the pleasure principle when an external object is out of reach. A corresponding phenomenon of mourning may be noted in the course of normal growth when a child or adolescent relinquishes childhood objects. Freud (1914) observed that "as libidinal interest is withdrawn from the love object into the ego, there is a damming up of libido in the ego. With this increase in tension, pain is experienced" (p. 101). Fantasies and daydreams that are not dependent on the existence of a real object may enter the mourning process in accordance with the pleasure principle, and may bind libido, as in some disturbed mourning processes they may continue to exist in the form of unassimilated and unintegrated introjects with which the mourner can carry on an inner conversation. Such an interrupted mourning process has an impoverishing effect on narcissism, since a fantasy object cannot reinforce the secondary narcissism of the mourner in the way a real love object does, nor can it function in an emotionally enriching way as does an internalized object. When the love object is already dead, but the mourning process has not yet included internalization of or identification with it, the mourner has recurrent dreams of a continuing coexistence with the lost object (Freud, 1911).

Later on, the pain of mourning lessens when longing for the object wanes, as a result of the withdrawal of libido. Ambivalent emotions toward the object then take its place. The mourner then approaches the conflicting emotions toward the lost object, aware of them either consciously or unconsciously. These contradictory emotions are connected with aggressions and death wishes. The belief in the magic power of death wishes may give rise to self-accusations and a sense of wickedness that lead to neurotic solutions or to depression if the object, a beloved person, is already dead, and therefore does not support the secondary narcissism of the mourner with libidinal object love.

The mourning process of the dying person himself often stops at this point, when, after painful mourning, both object libido and narcissistic libido have been withdrawn from active life and from the sick body into fantasies of life after death, and aggressions are directed by a splitting mechanism at everything that is lost and at the libidinal interest of fantasies (see Chapter 1). The mourning process of the dying person is arrested at this stage if introjection of the lost object with the aid of psychotherapy, or through otherwise favorable circumstances, is not possible.

The third phase of the mourning process is connected with *separation* from the lost object, when irreversible loss has become a reality and is no longer denied by fantasies about the present or the future. Separation activates past experiences of separation and the mechanisms used for their solution; it is therefore dependent on the subject's total personality, and is thus extremely individual. As has already been mentioned, object constancy attained in childhood determines the capacity for separation at a later time. Pollock (1961) points out that, in the separation of mourning, "The representation of the lost object is recathected because the instinctual energies that could have been discharged in actual relationship to the object, being now undischarged, recathect the internalized object image" (p. 349). Internalization takes place via introjection and identification. Freud said that identification with a lost object occurs through the "introjection of it into the ego." We assume that "identification is the earliest and original form of emotional tie" with an object. Thus "in a regressive way it becomes a substitute for a libidinal object-tie" by introjection (1921, pp. 107-109).

Separation anxiety stirs up hatred, and if separation is experienced as a significant narcissistic offense it arouses narcissistic rage in questions like: "Why is this happening to me?" "Why can't I do something about this?" "Who is doing this to me?" A childhood narcissistic trauma may later become an unavoidable obstruction to successful mourning work after the loss of an important object. In this connection, Kernberg (1974) observes that in the analysis of a narcissistic personality "the persistent absence of separation anxiety or mourning reactions" is striking, and that, instead, the void is filled by grandiose fantasies of the analyst and the self.

In the foregoing, the stages of the mourning process that cause emotions like shock, grief, pain, separation, and decathexis of the object have been dealt with. The last stage of the process is that of *adaptation:* adapting oneself to new, changed circumstances. This involves protracted mourning work during which the loss is integrated into the total personality in every respect, including the reactions of aggression. Mourning is a very personal process, depending on the subject's past experiences, his personality, his developmental stage and, lastly, on the narcissistic and the object-libidinal cathexis of the lost object. Integration of the changes brought about by the loss is not too complicated at an age and in conditions when libido can be provided with a satisfactory new object. The new object does not equal the lost one, which is not forgotten (except in early infancy); instead, it is a new human relationship. Finding new libidinal gratification, and through it new narcissistic gratification in place of the lost gratification, appears to be indispensable for mourning to be brought to an end.

Especially at an older age, and in losing a genital-level object who has been narcissistically very significant as well — such as one's own child, spouse, or work — bringing mourning to an end may meet with many obstacles. It may be manifest in a parent's difficulty in realizing that he or she is no longer indispensable to a grown-up child who has become independent. It is equally manifest in the recurrent dreams of the mourning period, when the genital-level object, now dead, is seen to be in need of care and help, even after the mourner's need to obtain object-libidinal gratification has been worked through during mourning. The last and the most difficult emotion to be worked through and integrated is the narcissistic blow of having become worthless to the lost object.

4.

On the Defensive Nature of Phallicity

THE PHALLOCENTRIC CONCEPTION

The phallocentric conception of the child's psychosexual development was early criticized by Jones (1933), Horney (1926, 1932), and Klein (1928), who conceived of phallicism as a secondary defensive construction. This opinion has received increasing current support, although from varying points of view. An illustrative viewpoint has been expressed by Schafer in his paper on "Problems in Freud's Psychology of Women" (1974), in which he inspected Freud's phallocentric conception in the light of later ego psychology, and arrived at the following conclusion about the child's psychosexual development: "No longer is ours a theory simply of instinct-ridden organisms, turbulent unconscious dynamics, and the like. We see all aspects of development as being profoundly influenced by learning in a context of object relations that are, on the one hand, biologically essential and biologically directed and, on the other hand, culturally molded and historically conditioned" (p. 459). It is only reasonable to take these facts into consideration in the following observations on the existence of woman's inner space.

According to the phallocentric conception, the main eroto-

Co-authored with Vilja Hägglund and Pentti Ikonen.

genic areas are the penis in boys and the clitoris in girls. When interest in the genitals awakens, it leads to the discovery of the difference between male and female genitals. This discovery is followed by the conception that the real genitals are the masculine ones, and that there is something amiss in the feminine counterpart or that they are nonexistent. The vagina and the womb are generally not known to exist, or they are considered unimportant.

A child is able to achieve a sensation of sexual pleasure and to lessen his sexual tension by the use of his hands or by tactile stimulation of his genitals in some other way. It is apparent that in the very beginning sexual excitation of the genitals aims at stimulation and acquisition of the accompanying pleasurable sensation. But even though the experience of stimulation and satisfaction becomes stronger and more distinct, the child does not understand the underlying impulses. They are reflected in his mind in a desire to do something forceful, to thrust into, to break into pieces, to tear a hole in something. Any effort to grasp the meaning of sexual intercourse is blocked by ignorance of the vagina (Freud, 1908b). But even though a child, from his limited viewpoint, conceives of the sexual act incorrectly, his desire still culminates in a wish to beget a child—a vague wish to impregnate and to become pregnant (Freud, 1924, 1926b). Thrusting into, tearing to pieces, tearing a hole in something, etc., are the aims of active phallic impulses, whereas becoming the object of these impulses or submitting to them is the aim of passive phallic drives. —The wish to have someone stimulate the genital erotogenic zone can be also regarded as a passive phallic aim. Similarly, the wish to become pregnant can be conceived of as a passive wish contrasting with the active wish to impregnate. The puzzling genitals, which are a source of pleasure as well as of anxiety in the phallic phase, induce in the child a desire to examine them, to exhibit them with the purpose of impressing others, and to find out the impression they make.

The object of the drive impulses in the phallic phase is the oedipal object, the parents. The earlier two-person relationship is now replaced by the relationship of three, in which the child experiences the other parent as an obstacle in the way of his wishes. This in turn leads to hostility toward the parent felt to be an obstacle, bringing on the fear of punishment and revenge directed specifically at the organs of phallic oedipal impulses, namely, the genitals. By these means the specific anxiety of the phallic phase gains intensity and leads to castration anxiety, which has its roots in the misconception of the difference between the male and the female sexual organs, the latter being seen as inferior or totally missing. Castration anxiety is also intensified by the passive phallic wishes that contain the fantasy of mutilation of the sexual organ.

Additional proof to a child for having to fear castration seems to be the child's general belief that a larger organ is better than a small one, and that there are more advantages in urinating with a penis than with the female organ.

It is obvious that all the so-called phallic fantasies, whatever other factors they may contain, can be understood as a defense against castration anxiety. Different as these fantasies may be otherwise — active, passive, or whatever — they all contain as a common element the fantasy of a phallus that is invincible in its function. Phallic, however, is not the equivalent of masculine, nor is feminine its opposite — rather, it is castrated. Creatures regarded as masculine as well as feminine can be both phallic and castrated — fairy tales and dreams provide ample examples. A gun as a phallic symbol is very expressive, but it is a poor representative of the timid, erect penis not fit to be any kind of weapon; yet it represents well the castrating phallus and the invincible phallus defying castration.

There is a feature of the adult sexual act, genital intercourse, that from the behavioristic standpoint fits the phallic fantasies well. Sexual intercourse — the behavioristic view has it as the penis penetrating the vagina — requires the erection or activity of the male genital, but not that of the female genital. Besides the fact that the female, because of her body structure, cannot phallicly penetrate the male during intercourse, she seems to be destined to a partially dependent and passive role during the act owing to the lack of a phallus. The function of the penis dictates the course of the sexual act, and the reactions of the female are of no importance. In the extreme case the male can even resort to force. By behavioristic standards this is called intercourse, but in the analytical view it is an experience of phallic violence.

In principle, a man has the possibility of realizing active phallic fantasies in a way that outwardly resembles genital intercourse, whereas a woman lacks that possibility, and this fact tends strongly to support phallic fantasies on the adult level. The phallic helplessness of the woman *de facto,* so to speak, is fertile ground from which spring numerous fantasies of women as the lesser, the weaker, and the passive sex.

Phallic fantasies thus originate in the misconception of the sexual impulses connected with excitation of a child's genital zone. These fantasies function on the one hand as the source of castration anxiety, and on the other hand as a defense against it. Castration anxiety is further enforced and maintained by the fear of punishment and revenge brought about by the oedipal conflict. (In this connection the forerunners of castration anxiety connected with earlier developmental stages may be left out of the discussion.)

The inability to understand sexual impulses in the genital sense is the result of the fact that a child is unaware of the existence and/or function of the vagina. Developmentally he is not yet mature enough for this, nor can his own observations or information available provide him with the knowledge his own psychophysical being is as yet unable to offer.

The question can be asked, however, whether such a stubborn inability to conceive of the existence and the meaning of the vagina is based only on the psychosexual immaturity of the child in the phallic phase, or whether there are other factors to be taken into account. The child does have fantasies of pregnancy and of impregnation in this phase that are in no way related to his realistic psychophysical possibilities at that age. Could it be that the child, by means of his phallic fantasies, defends himself not only against the incomprehensibility of new sexual impulses, and the castration anxiety that follows misconception of these impulses, but also against consciousness of the vagina, the womb, and the female inner space with all the problems involved?

THE INNER SPACE CONCEPTION

The infant's experience of oral gratification via the mother or mother substitute is the prototype of all two-person relationships to follow. The drive gratification supplied by oral erotogenic zones, in addition to the experience of intimacy, which for the child means the mother's care via the mouth, the skin, and the senses, contains even the experience of the inner space. The child takes and receives warm milk into his oral inner space, and the emptiness of his inner space distresses him with the sensation of hunger. Freud (1905) expressed the view that in the oral psychosexual stage, when sexual activity has not yet become separate from taking nourishment, the child incorporates objects cannibalistically. This is the archaic prototype of later identification, which, however, is not as total. The experience of the *oral inner space* means introjection of the object *in toto,* devouring the object, keeping it in the inner space, etc. The object of love, hate, or ambivalent emotions is incorporated into the oral inner space. The object then no longer exists outside the subject as a separate part or entity.

Before the anal psychosexual developmental stage, the child has incorporated, i.e., introjected by oral mechanisms, the caring and frustrating mother. He has introjected the prototype of love and hate in the two-person relationship. When the mother has been experienced mainly as the source of care and gratification, the child also develops a desire to care and to give from his own inner space. The libidinal experience of the *anal inner space,* again, is the wish to retain, on the one hand, the narcissistically cathected content of the bowels, and on the other, to give it to the mother. The child is then identified, in part, with the oral giver, the mother, and on his part now gives the mother his anal product. To some degree, the child has the experience of caring for and loving the object of the anal phase, which is the precursor of caring for the object of the genital level, and from which later evolves the sublimated desire to care for, to organize, to keep clean and in order, and to be regular.

The anal object has been formed in the anal inner space; it is the intermediary form between the subject and the object, being partly cathected narcissistically and partly by object libido. There is a significant difference between the child's experience of the oral phase and that of the anal one, in that in the anal phase the child has a narcissistically cathected object in his own inner space, and he can share it only by giving it to his mother and by getting the measure of his narcissistic value in his mother's reactions. Passing the anal inner space object on to another becomes the basic model for giving and receiving joy and pleasure by means of a *mutually shared object.* In the oral phase mutuality is experienced in the *shared emotion of merging,* in the "oceanic" feeling of fusion, and in mother's warmth, in her milk, and in her loving care, which have all become fused with the child's existence.

When, by the end of the anal phase, the child has had the experiences of oral introjection and anal giving or, in other words, the mystery of giving from and accepting into his own inner space, he has also outgrown the experience of the mother as part of himself, and has now acquired the knowledge that the mother is something separate and outside himself. With omnipotent fantasies he tries to hold onto the belief that the mother can be governed by the same means that he uses to govern parts of his own body or its functions. He then gradually becomes more aware of the mother's true nature in their interrelations. The mother's genital-level care and concern have continuously been aimed at him, but not until now does he realize that they are part of the mother's nature. The process of growing up then impels the child to internalize the mother and to identify with her. This is experienced by the child as impinging on his very existence, unlike the earlier experiences that affected only the object of anal inner space. In other words, the child is able to perceive the sublimated aspects of the mother's genital-level libidinal inner space, but he does not understand the mechanism of the inner space. A comparison could be made to the child's falling in love with warm wind, and desiring to possess its very existence without in the least grasping what makes the wind blow.

In Winnicott's (1953) presentation of the transitional phenomenon, mother and child's mutual illusion — the reality of emotion — of the transitional object affords the child the possibility of experiencing that the mother-child relationship continues in relation to the transitional object. Thus is the basis formed for the individual ability to relate to external reality in a creative, preserving way, and in a way that unites people (Hägglund, 1974). This becomes possible when the child is content and free from instinctual tension. Driven by his instincts a child tries in one way or another to obtain instinctual gratification from his mother or to identify with and internalize the gratifying mother. If the mother cannot satisfy the child's needs and if identification with her proves impossible, the child in his frustration aims his hatred at her. By becoming like the mother, the child can himself become the provider of drive gratification to himself and to others. The way in which a child is able to identify with the mother in the anal and oedipal phases appears to a great extent to be dependent on the prevailing environmental and familial culture.

A little girl can identify with her mother most fully in favorable conditions and can internalize the qualities of motherhood. Among these are carrying a child in her inner genital space, giving birth to a child from the inner space, and caring for the child; furthermore, they include the mother's sublimated inner space qualities, such as taking care of the home and its surroundings. Through identification, a child can sometimes experience a likeness to the mother, and in this way can continue the mother-child relationship as the other partner, the mother. Erikson (1951) has described how a girl's inner space fantasies are reflected in her play. He has come to the conclusion that a girl's play is based on decidedly feminine elements; in other words, on the existence of the specifically female organ in which to keep and to hold, into which to shut, and in which to care for and protect the genital-level object.

A little girl does not, of course, possess a developed and complete inner genital space, which is developed only in adolescence. Not until puberty do the girl's ovulation and menses and the boy's ejaculation make procreation and budding generativity possible. Before that time, phenomena like procreation and generativity are within the reach of a child's fantasy through bits of knowledge learned from adults, and through identification with parents in constant mutual relations. It is clear that in cultures where the female inner space is veiled in obscurity, the child's conception of the mother's sexuality will differ from that of a child brought up in a culture that allows him to participate in the sublimated and social forms of generativity through optimum ways of knowing and understanding. Sharing genital inner space experience with a child thus takes place on a more developed level than in the anal phase yet in the same way, by means of a mutually shared object. The mutual object is now *a shared illusion of the child in the mother's inner space,* an impression of reality created by a mutual illusion. In the oral phase there is then a shared emotion of merging, in the anal phase there is a shared object, but in the *child's genital phase* there is a shared illusion. A child has no possibility of experiencing fusion in sexual intercourse; he possesses neither the physical nor the psychic ability for it. In fact, a child has very little interest in the experience of his parents' orgasm; his interest lies in masturbatory caressing and in the mystery of the mother's inner space.

When a small child, or even a somewhat older child, instead of sharing motherhood through identification becomes only its object and dependent on the mother, then motherhood leads to emotions of envy from which it is difficult to find the way out. When a small child contemplates the bliss of motherhood and the creative elation in the relationship between the mother and the baby, or when he observes the sublimated inner space qualities of the mother, his envy encompasses both the object of motherly care and the mother herself. The envy aroused by motherhood is the first and strongest emotion of envy the child experiences, and it is aimed at the very person he is dependent on. Through identification with the mother, both boys and girls are able to participate in what, to a certain degree, they envy. Part of the envy leads to efforts to neutralize the aggressions caused by it, or to efforts to destroy the cause. In the oedipal phase the ego of the child is still weak and immature and needs continual support by the environment, particularly the mother, in order to cope with the problems of envy by way of psychic growth and identification. If the child is left alone with his mother envy, or if the defense mechanisms that obstruct identification with motherhood are overvalued, the child will unconsciously be on the defensive against envy and ensuing conflicts. Mother envy will, in the unconscious, then lead to constant defensive attitudes and to later diffi-

culties in adopting the various qualities of genital-level parent-
hood.

The difficulty a child has in understanding the functions of
the mother's inner space is connected not only with his as yet
undeveloped ability to procreate but also with the mother's
need to protect her inner space against envy, as well as the
difficulty she encounters in trying to describe to the child her
inner space in a way he can grasp. It is similarly difficult for
the mother to describe experiences of pregnancy and intercourse to the envious child, and therefore she rationalizes her
inability by shyness or by remarks about the child's limited
understanding of such matters. Mothers often find it easier to
describe genital inner space functions to girls, with whom they
more easily identify, than to boys. Mothers are more afraid of
little boys' aggressive fantasies and envy despite the fact that
they rationally recognize the harmlessness and sexual incapacity of little boys. The difficulties a child encounters in
trying to understand the mother's genital inner space may
easily lead to interpretations that are in accord with the child's
own experiences of inner space, with accompanying over-
emphasis of oral and anal elements as well as features of
childhood genital masturbation.

The genital inner space experiences of adulthood are based
not on the instinctual strivings or aims of any specific erotogenic zone in relation to a part object, but rather on the
relation between the total personality and the total object.
This object relation is already partially developed in the
infancy of both girls and boys by way of identification. In a
woman motherhood develops partially alongside of physical
and psychic growth, and it finds fulfillment in the relationship
between two persons with a child. As a libidinal instinct
motherhood has the extraordinary quality in both animals and
humans of embracing even the young of alien species. A she-
cat, for instance, will carry food to a crying human baby, and
a kitten awakens motherly instincts in human beings. Mother-

hood, then, is a quality that is more prominent in women than in men, but it is nevertheless not completely bound to sex or to species. Fatherhood, too, contains sublimated inner space qualities. Through identification with qualities of his mother and father, a boy develops the desire and the ability to impregnate the inner space and to care for the child in woman's inner space. It is a mutual experience, a mutually shared illusion, an emotional reality. It is the foundation on which the boy develops in himself the sublimated qualities of care and concern.

Identification with motherhood in the mother-child relationship is a completely different function from identification with the mother who is the father's sexual partner and who takes the father's sexual organ into her own. Gratification of drive impulses relates to intercourse in a different way than to motherhood and fatherhood. Genital drive gratification in intercourse is linked with the orgastic experience in the genitals. It has developed from the partial drive gratification of childhood masturbation of the erotogenic areas to the orgastic experience of adults of two sexes with the penis and the clitoris-vagina as the erotogenic zones.

The orgastic potential of adulthood, however, does not always develop in conjunction with the genital inner space function. The parents' orgastic gratification does not intrigue the child as does their mutual genital inner space gratification. Although inner space is in close contact with the sexual organs, it does not include gratification of orgastic impulses. The genital inner space has a function only in relation to a real partner. The function of the inner space as a generative phenomenon can be realized only with another person. Contrarily, it is possible to achieve orgastic gratification on one's own with the aid of a fantasy. The goal of inner space function is always the well-being of another person. Orgastic gratification, on the contrary, is accomplished in the personal psychophysical system regardless of the well-being of another person, or even in opposition to it. If a child never becomes acquainted with the reality and the meaning of the inner space, his efforts to solve the mystery will turn his attention to the contiguous problem of the pleasure attained in intercourse and in stimulation of erotogenic zones. Genital inner space then acquires qualities of the erotogenic zone that are oral, anal, urethral, or genitomasturbatory in nature.

PHALLICITY AS A NEUROTIC COMPROMISE

Jones (1933) presented a phallocentric view that differed from Freud's conception. Jones considered phallicity not as a developmental phase, but as a defense reaction and a neurotic compromise: "Both sexes strive against accepting the belief in the second class, and both for the same reason — namely, from a wish to disbelieve in the supposed reality of castration" (p. 453). He described two separate psychic processes of the phallic phase. The first is the *protophallic phase* when the child supposes that all other people are sexually like him. There are the penis and the clitoris, the sources of masturbatory pleasure, but questions about the difference between the sexes do not arise. The second is the *deuterophallic phase* when the child divides people into two separate classes, not so much into men and women as into the penis-possessing and the castrated. According to Jones, this phase is more neurotic than the first one, because it contains a conflict, anxiety, striving to accept the supposed castration as a reality, and in addition the boys' overcompensation of the narcissistic value of the penis, and the girls' fantasies of mingled hope and despair. Jones describes the deuterophallic phase as follows:

> It is less sadistic, the main relic of this being a tendency to ominpotence phantasies; and it is more self-centred, the chief allo-erotic attribute still remaining, being its exihibitionistic aspect. It is thus less aggressive and less related to other people, notably to women. How has this change been

brought about? It would seem to be changed in the direction of phantasy and away from the real world of contact with other human beings. If so, this would in itself justify a suspicion that there is a flight element present, and that we have not to do simply with a natural evolution towards greater reality and a more developed adjustment [p. 482].

Jones comes to the conclusion that

the previous heterosexual allo-erotism of the early phase is in the deutero-phallic one — in both sexes — largely transmuted into a substitutive homosexual auto-erotism. This latter phase would thus — in both sexes — be not so much a pure libidinal development as a neurotic compromise between libido and anxiety, between the natural libidinal impulses and the wish to avoid mutilation [p. 483].

The defensive quality of phallicity leads to an isolated existence for the person, who finds greatest security in phallic fantasies and their derivatives. Phallic fantasies are steered away from the genital inner space and its derivatives because they are experienced as a threat to the constancy of the fantasies. A child, in the prephallic phase of development, has therefore partly abandoned the libidinal affection for his parents. This has not taken place by way of separation-individuation (Mahler, 1968), with the internalization of parents who provide security and ego strength, and who pass on their abilities to the child. The process is rather one of flight from one's own castration fantasy to another fantasy, the fantasy of a phallus that withstands mutilation, and that, by its power, controls the castrating features seen in the parents. The genital phase of childhood is not tantamount to the phallic phase as a phase of development. When a child's genitality is budding and he is unable to integrate it into his personality on his own, it is defensively transformed into a phallic quality.

PHALLICITY AS A DEFENSIVE ORGANIZATION

According to Mahler (1968), the symbiotic phase of the mother-child relationship is followed by the separation-individuation process. Transference of libido first goes through a "hatching" process, a phase of maturation, when the child's interest is directed at the environment and then at the mother, especially at her face and her expressions. The child gets acquainted with his surroundings, simultaneously combining his observations with observations of his mother in a "checking back" fashion. The mother functions as an auxiliary ego to the child with regard to the impulses and traumas outside the symbiotic mother-child relationship. The hatching process is followed by a passing over of the massive libidinal cathexis from the symbiotic area to the autonomous apparatuses of the self and to ego functions like locomotion, perception, and learning. In other words, the child now becomes a little individual, finding reflections of himself and his perceivable environment in the mother's face. During the phase of individuation a child adopts speech as a means of communication between himself and his mother. After the shared physical unity and interrelations of the oral phase, the mutual perceptions of mother and child are shifted to an external anal object cathected by both. This is followed by a shifting of the cathexis to perceptions of the external world shared by mother and child, and finally to *verbal communication* in which a word uttered by the mother is strongly cathected.

On this basis, it is not difficult to understand the meaning of the libidinally cathected verbal interrelations between mother and child by the time the child reaches the oedipal age and his interest is drawn to the mysteries of sexual activity. If the family culture has adopted an "inheritance" from forebears of denying children the possibility of verbally sharing the secrets of the genital inner space and the possibility of experiencing them together with their parents, then the result may well resemble a situation in which the mother withdraws from interrelations and conceals her emotional reactions toward the child's anal object or oral interaction. It is not only the concrete genitals of his parents that form the object of the child's genital phase; even inspection of them is of little help to him in understanding the mystery of the inner space. The object of the child's genital phase is a *created object*. It is an illusion created by both child and parent evolved like the illusion presented by Winnicott (1953; 1971; see also Hägglund, 1974). In the mother's company the child creates an illusion of the inner space, the reality of which is perceived by both, and the child shares the illusion and the understanding conveyed by it with the mother whose function is that of an auxiliary ego for the child. Where creative interaction is missing the child will develop his own libidinal fantasies and even fantasies of fear which closely follow oral, anal, and urethral patterns familiar to the child.

When a child cannot grasp the idea of the inner space, and because he is afraid of being excluded from the unknown, in his loneliness he begins to form phallic fantasies. These fantasies are derived from earlier fantasies of omnipotence. The child defensively transfers the omnipotent fantasies of the symbiotic phase to the genital area of childhood, where they have the context of himself in relation to his own phallic image instead of the earlier meaning of omnipotent unity between mother and child. In his phallic fantasies the child with his phallus has the power, the omnipotence, and the security he had in the earlier symbiotic mother-child relationship. Just as in that phase deprivation of the mother was a threat, so in the present phase deprivation of the phallus threatens in the form of castration anxiety. The phallus becomes a magic wand which in the child's fantasies is totally his own, as his mother was in the symbiotic phase, and never becomes a threat by cooperating with a threatening force. Thus it can be understood that, setting aside everything else, phallic narcissism offers the child narcissistic support in the imperfection of primary narcissism.

In the genital phase of infancy, the phallus becomes a savior from the horrors of the fear of loneliness. As a result of growth, the child partly abandons his mother and individuates, but if lack of verbal communication curtails his understanding of motherhood and/or fatherhood in terms of the genital inner space, he turns to his father in his disappointment with his mother; he invests the male sex with magical phallic qualities, which now acquire the features and the function of the male genitals, hypercathected by exaggerated features of the phallus. The phallic fantasy has its origin in the mother-child relationship, corresponding to the magic-omnipotent mother or the mother-child unity. The imaginary phallus becomes a giant nipple that gives comfort, a magic wand that fends off hunger, fear, and despair. It is an exaggerated "auxiliary ego" for the child, to compensate for his smallness, his imperfection, and his inability to cope alone, and to give him a magical sense of power.

Investing greater power in the phallic fantasy means greater security against the magic-omnipotent mother when the child has abandoned the mother-child symbiosis. In the child's imagination the phallic mother may correspond to his own fearful phallic, anal, or oral images. Like a monster raised by any of these fears, she invades the inner space of the child or of someone else, depending on whether the child has internalized or externalized her. The phallic mother, who is best symbolized by the witch in fairy tales, is a sum of all the images the child has of the aggressions he has accumulated toward the mother in the pregenital developmental phases. By the mechanism of splitting the child forms two mother images, of whom the one is an orally good mother, anally participating in and sharing the child's genital illusions, and the other her opposite, corresponding to the child's hateful image of the mother-witch. With the transfer of the mother's magic power to the phallic fantasy, ambivalence follows and with it a split. This makes the child feel better in the sense that the fearfulness of his aggressions lessens. While the content of oral hate has been the desire to destroy with voracity and the fear of the self being eaten, and the content of anal hate the desire to push away altogether or to imprison and the fear of the self being the victim of these emotions, phallic hate is less total. It is restricted to castration of the genitals or penetration of the object, thereby indicating only the wish to castrate/penetrate, not to kill. This does not mean, of course, that hate directed at an object could not begin with phallic castration or penetration and then be transformed into more total destruction.

The defensive nature of phallicity is also reflected in the leaning on old patterns of drive solutions of the very earliest mother-child relationship, and the transferring of them as such into another context, into phallic fantasies to build up a defense against drive conflict. In other words, it could be said, "old wine in new bottles." Phallicity is rather more like a defensive structure than a mere defensive reaction. According to van der Leeuw (1958), a defensive structure can be understood as "an associated and related corpus of instinctive impulses, affects, feelings and defence reactions, which together serve to keep certain feelings, instinctive impulses, affects and experiences remote from the ego, because the individual mechanisms fail to do so. The intensities are too great, and it requires an organization to bring about and maintain the defense" (p. 112).

In addition to the impulses that emanate from the drives, the ego must defend itself against the phallic demands of the superego. Insofar as these are tied up with the ego ideal, the individual must exert himself to realize the phallic expectations of the ego ideal from which phallic morality has developed. The phallic ethos has both an active and a passive component: power, force, and honor—submission, sacrifice, and veneration. Its opposite is identification with the good,

gentle giver and carer. The phallic structure has probably
been formed mainly as a protection against the child's envy of
the genital inner space and its derivatives.

PHALLIC DEFENSIVE ORGANIZATION
AGAINST INNER SPACE ENVY

When an infant becomes aware of the genital inner space
and his parents' libidinal interest in it, as well as of their
creative joy, he feels envious. The envy is provoked by seeing
the mother lovingly cherish a baby at her breast, by the picture
of the parents loving each other in a genital embrace, and by
the picture of the father loving the baby in the genital inner
space. The child is aware of the various parts of the inner space
but he is unable to put the pieces together without the creative
illusion mentioned earlier. The creative illusion makes it
possible for the child to share the reality of, be a part of, as a
child, his parents' genital inner space and its various derivatives as represented in the spirit of the home. When creative
illusion is not enough, the child has no choice but to resolve his
feelings of being an outsider and his emotions of envy by other
means. The child is aware that he is not yet able to be an adult
sexually, and that he is forbidden to enter into his parents'
relationship; he is, therefore, narcissistically offended.

If the genital inner space is regarded as only the erotogenic
zone and the manifestation of drive pleasure belonging to an
adult woman's genital sexuality, and not as the joint "grain
field" of a man and a woman, then it is obvious that there is a
great difference between the reactions to it of boys and girls. In
every respect still immature and powerless, girls may resort to
masochistic means to solve the problem. Masochistic means
are adopted by the weak child who, by flinging accusations at
them, tries to reach his parents, whom he feels are overwhelm-
ingly his superiors. Girls may react like boys by turning their
backs on the inner space because when they feel it is out of

their reach, they are narcissistically wounded. A phallic defensive organization is then substituted. After this, defense is the more pronounced the fewer inner space derivatives the child perceives in his father. The support and sense of security given to his son by a father does not have to be phallic or phallic-narcissistic; it can simply be narcissistic. It is then that a boy can identify with the father who takes care of the derivatives of a woman's inner space and his offspring with the satisfaction derived from generativity. Through identification with such a father a boy finds it possible to identify with his mother as well.

Jacobson (1950) has set forth the view that a boy, too, cherishes the wish to give birth to a child, and that there are certain men, very often creatively talented, whose feminine qualities are fixated to the jealousy they feel toward pregnant and childbearing women. She claims that it would seem that creative work and creativity normally can supply a man with the possibility of realizing, by way of sublimation, the wish to carry a child and to give birth. Similarly van der Leeuw (1958), on the basis of case histories, has presented a man's reactions when he acknowledges this inability to bear children like a mother as follows: "The obstacles to be overcome are the feelings of rage, jealousy, rivalry, and above all of impotence and helplessness and the destructive aggression which accompany these experiences. Child-bearing is experienced as achievement, power, and competition with the mother. It is an identification with the active producing mother" (p. 115).

In summary, it can be said that the means used by a child faced with mother envy are aimed at his own emotions or at the envied motherhood. A child can deal with his envy in a way that *preserves* his emotions as well as the object, by identification with motherhood directly or through his father's emotions of generativity. Additionally, by sharing mother's and father's inner space illusion he can become part of it. Finally, however, his inner space experiences will come to mature fulfillment only after adolescence. Whenever the resolution of identification or creativity is impossible, the child will aim his aggressive emotions at the envied motherhood or will change his world of values by the phallic defensive organization. When aggressions are aimed directly at the envied motherhood, the child will strive, by prephallic mechanisms, to destroy totally the emotion of envy, its object, or its source. The phallic defensive organization against the child's own envious emotions is in this respect more object preserving because phallic aggression does not totally destroy, does not kill, it only *mutilates,* castrates. In this sense phallic defensive organization is more object and culture preserving when possibilities of identification and creativity are restricted, as they apparently are more or less. The phallic defensive organization is harmful to the child's development only if it is put forth as an ideal or an aim by the surrounding culture or the parent figures. The harm is done because phallicity in its defensive aim puts restrictions on the individual personality, narrows it by thrusting motherhood and creativity under phallic control as secondary functions.

5.

Mourning and Creativity

CREATIVITY AS AN ARTISTIC AND
A SCIENTIFIC MANIFESTATION

Creativity has traditionally been regarded as embodied in artistic phenomena, and people who express themselves by artistic means are regarded as having *creative personalities.* Work in the various fields of science is also considered creative, and it may be said that creativity is understood to be an act of creating—of bringing to be—something new, or at least of aspiring to do so. In studies of creative personalities, the approach has been one of diagnostically inspecting the complexity of their problems and contending that creativity is applicable to the resolution of intrapsychic conflicts, or that as a result of fixations and regression in psychosexual development creative talent is conflict-ridden. When the personalities of creative people are inspected from this point of view, a hypothesis of healthy or unhealthy creativity is arrived at. Creativity can then be expressive of a *regressive process of illness,* as, for instance, in the painting or poem of a schizophrenic patient, or it is the activity of the *healthy part of the personality,* which is separate from the process of the illness. Taking the life situation, the human relationships, and the conflicts of creative people as a starting point, analyses have been carried out on Leonardo da Vinci (Freud, 1910), Dostoevsky

109

(Freud, 1928), Goethe (Eissler, 1963), Luther (Erikson, 1958), and many others by inspecting the products of their artistic or scientific creativity and the course of their life cycles.

It has been an established practice in psychoanalysis to point out similarities between the creative activity and some neurotic processes. An explanation could be found in the fact that, in a sense, there is a resemblance between neurotic fantasy and creative illusion. Freud (1908a) pointed out that certain aspects of literature and of paintings can be interpreted as fantasies of the oedipal phase, and that creativity has a resemblance to daydreams. Klein (1948) has contributed the viewpoint that creative activity is either depressive or schizoid, that it is either an effort at reparation of a person's own destructive fantasy, or comparable to a schizophrenic person's delusional system-making. These hypotheses do not, however, throw any light on the question why some people are able to find a creative solution for their neurotic, depressive, or schizoid problems.

A great many studies in the psychoanalytic literature indicate that an artistic product is the outcome of a later elaboration of a childhood fantasy (A. Freud, 1922; Kris, 1952, 1953; Sachs, 1942; Meyer and Blacher, 1960). According to these studies, creativity is a highly developed capacity of expression based on childhood experience. Kris (1952) writes that "creative inspiration is based on a process of projection and reintrojection which utilizes neutralized energy derived originally from breast hallucinations of the oral period and later homosexual conflicts." Thus the creativity of an artist's work originates in the mother-child relationship, and works of art reflect further the emotional bondage—and accompanying conflicts—to the male and to the father. Greenacre (1957, 1958, 1960) has also observed in her investigations of creative artists that creative inspiration has its roots in the experiences of the oral phase, and that an artist in his creative production seeks the "primitive oceanic feeling." On the other hand,

Greenacre holds that inspiration originates in the hopes and fantasies of the oedipal phase, when artistic inspiration is experienced as a divine gift, a gift from the father-god to the passive-feminine recipient, or else as an active-masculine "family romance."

Kris (1952) and Hartmann (1964) have described imaginative activity as an ego function and as regressive activity which is nevertheless creative and progressive in the sphere of the total personality. Kris (1953) examines creativity from the point of view of the creative process itself. He also mentions healthy creativity which is based on "regression in the service of the ego," or, in other words, on "controlled regression." The opposite of this is pathological creativity in which the regressive person cannot control his unconscious fantasies, which then invade the conscious in the form of primary-process thinking and are therefore considered absurd and hallucinatory from the point of view of the ego.

The definition of creative activity in itself already contains the idea of novelty, of something unexpected and therefore unpredictable. For this reason it is a difficult task to describe it in terms of psychoanalytic causality and determinism. Additional difficulties in understanding creativity come from the conflicting opinions about whether creativity should be regarded as a general attribute, the possession of anyone if and when inhibitions are not present, as Kubie (1958) has said, or should be considered the specific gift of a few talented people. Greenacre (1957) supports the latter opinion. She believes that talented people differ from others already in infancy, and are in active pursuit of human relations, of objects ready to recognize their exceptional talent.

In my opinion, artistic and scientific creativity should be carefully looked at apart from the person's other simultaneous goals and strivings inspired by his creatively active inspirations in arts or science. These other strivings may or may not be in harmony with one another. Besides indicating creativity, they can contain an expression of the person's unneutralized and unsublimated archaic narcissism, which constitutes the transformation of creativity. When creative expressions are strongly cathected narcissistically, they are protected and safe-guarded as though they were a living part of the person. Artistic and/or scientific expression can serve a person's needs to externalize or to project inner conflicts onto the external world with creative means and methods, thus making possible their solution as external conflicts, not as inner neurotic problems; this solution has already been hinted at earlier in the text. A person's socially utilitarian and ambitious goals can likewise steer his artistic or scientific activity.

I believe it is fruitful to undertake an exploration of the essence of creativity without linking it to any external activity or mode of action. Creativity is primarily an emotional, inner occurrence, although it finds an outlet in external forms through specific agents. A creative experience is as much a part of a peasant's day when he ploughs his grain fields as it is when he rests by the ditch and writes a poem about his work or paints a picture of it. The decisive difference is that in the latter case his conscious aim is to transmit the experience to someone else by illustrating it in words or paint.

CREATIVITY AS A "THING IN ITSELF"

Winnicott (1971) has examined creativity as a "thing in itself," and expresses it as follows:

> The creative impulse is therefore something that can be looked at as a thing in itself, something that of course is necessary if an artist is to produce a work of art, but also as something that is present when *anyone*—baby, child, adolescent, adult, old man or woman—looks in a healthy way at anything deliberately, such as making a mess with faeces or prolonging the act of crying to enjoy a musical

sound. It is present as much in the moment-by-moment living of a backward child who is enjoying breathing as it is in the inspiration of an architect who suddenly knows what it is that he wishes to construct, and who is thinking in terms of material that can actually be used so that his creative impulse may take form and shape, and the world may witness [p. 69].

Winnicott's (1953) observation that a close connection exists between the creative artist and the person admiring the created product in their reciprocal relationship to it led him to discover the "transitional object" and "transitional phenomenon." The transitional phase in a child's development is the phase when the infant withdraws from the dependent relationship to his mother or mother substitute in the two-person relationship and transfers part of his attachment to some other object. When that object is at hand, the child experiences security and warmth similar to what his mother's presence had earlier provided. The most striking example of the transitional object is a soft toy the child immediately turns to whenever he is sad or alone, and especially when he is going to sleep. He hugs the toy tightly and feels unity and security. According to Winnicott, this is a child's first creative attitude toward the environment. The child has created for himself a significant image of the object. Although the same object has been there before, it now becomes a valued thing because the child has invested it with an image his emotions have created. The created image is no hallucinatory delusion, it is part of the environment that the child has endowed with his subjective imaginary picture, and thus the transitional object becomes an intermediary form between an illusion and a real object. As the child grows, the transitional object as such loses its meaning while real object relations gain in importance.

However, the transitional object and the experiences of the transitional phase play an important part in a child's play, in an adult's creative work, in appreciation of works of art, etc. They are the foundation of all creative activity. The creative ability acquired during the transitional phase is, of course, subject to development, and therefore later relationships of two are likely to intensify and renew the creative talent. For instance, a person who falls deeply in love experiences creativity more intensely than before. Similarly, the loss of an important object in childhood or later in life may activate the latent potentials of the transitional phase; creativity plays an important part in the mourning work that follows a loss (see Chapter 2).

CREATIVITY AS AN INTROJECTED HUMAN RELATIONSHIP

In the transitional phase, the child creates an image of the inanimate object, and it is the product of his imagination or *an illusion of the reality of emotion.* The mother or mother substitute shares the transitional phase illusion with the child; the child hugs his pillow or his Teddy bear, and the mutual illusion of child and mother is that the "Teddy bear, too, likes the child." This is not a delusion but instead creative play; neither one believes in the reality of the situation, yet their mutual illusion about the Teddy bear joins them in the reality of the illusion, thus expelling the feeling of loneliness. Some years later, the child will play in his mother's presence with his toy cars, and the illusion of the play is that he imagines himself to be driving a car on the city streets. The mother attends to her own household duties at the same time, absorbed in her own thoughts. The child has now internalized the ability to play, and he enjoys himself in the playful, creative illusion of being alone in the presence of another human being, his mother. According to Winnicott (1958), there is, in addition to the three-person relationship and two-person relationship, the relationship to being alone. He observes that "the ability to be truly alone has as its basis the early experience of being alone in the presence of someone. Being alone in the presence of someone can take place at a very early stage, when the ego immaturity is naturally balanced by ego-support from the mother. In the course of time the individual introjects the ego-supportive mother and in this way becomes able to be alone without frequent reference to the mother or mother symbol" (p. 32).

The ability that is born in the transitional phase and is later developed to create an illusion of an object or an event, to share the experience as an emotional reality with another, and to experience the joy of creating in solitude because one has internalized a safe and secure relationship in childhood—that ability, in a nutshell, is the capacity to relate creatively to the environment. It is a function of the ego, which radiates a feeling of ego unity between individuals in their social inter-relations, unlike the instinctual relationship in which the gratification of drives is in the forefront. Here lies the basis for the fact that creative attitudes toward other people, toward animate or inanimate nature, vanish when the need for drive gratification reaches a certain intensity, and the mutually shared creative illusion is displaced by the desire to discharge drive tension. Drive gratification is experienced as a silent and peaceful event in relation to both libidinal and aggressive instincts. Not until drive equilibrium has been attained in one way or another, or its attainment has been guaranteed, can the individual relate to his environment in a creative way. A guarantee of drive equilibrium is the trust in environmental good will acquired in infancy through "good enough mothering," and in later years, in adolescence and in adulthood, by benevolent human relations. This trust develops from recurrent and sufficient drive gratification. Not until then can creativity emerge as an ego function characteristic of the individual. The inspirational content of creativity is enthusiasm, and the creative accomplishment contains the emotion of joy,

a feeling much more sublime than mere gaiety or the enjoyment of entertainment. The joy of accomplishment is the
joyous feeling that all goes well; in other words, the feeling of
wholesomeness and of health. It contains no passionate drive
desire, nor does it know hate or revenge for wounded self-
esteem, for in creativity these elements are dormant. When
one or another of them becomes imperative, the creative experience and its product are transformed. The goal then is no
longer the joy of creating, but rather the desire to change, to
mold, to control, and to possess.

CREATIVITY JOINS PEOPLE TOGETHER

Creativity, as far as I can see, is a different ego function
from the ego defense mechanisms. It is an ability born in the
primary two-person relationship, the one between mother and
child, in conjunction with the transitional phenomenon. It is
an ability developed alongside psychic growth to be benefited
by the ego as a characteristic feature of each developmental
stage. It binds two people together in a different way than does
a shared drive gratification, a shared object that has the
aim of advantageous, defensive, or narcissistic acquisition and
of heightened self-sufficiency. The prominent element in this
kind of creativity is not direct gratification of drive impulses, it
is rather the creative experience as a sublimated form of drives
uniting people who are able to kindle the emotional reality of a
mutual creative illusion.

Whenever creative ability in relation to shared illusion
proves insufficient, envy toward creative people or created
products is provoked, and the person attempts to free himself
of his envy by means that are not based on identification or on
a mutual creative illusion, such means being: ego defense
mechanisms; intentionally causing damage or destruction to
the object of envy; and gaining control of the object. Since
creativity is a value in itself, conveying pleasure, joy, health,

and peace of mind, it is understandable that, when creative illusion with its uniting capacity is absent, the person strives for its attainment by any *active* means within his reach, notwithstanding the fact that the experience of creativity is possible only in a passively experienced devotion to an external or an internalized object relation.

Passive devotion to creative experience has been described in various terms: "regression in the service of the ego" (Kris, 1953), "mystical experience" (Horton, 1974), "experience of inspiration" (Greenacre, 1957, 1958, 1960), and also in religious terms: "unity with God." It seems to me that there is a paradox in the creativity uniting people in that the road to progressive goals goes through regression. By regressing to experiences of the primary two-person relationship, the goal is to reach, by way of sublimation, the most socially developed and the most experientially rich forms of social communication, where ambivalence causes minimum disturbance. Muensterberger (1962) has presented the idea as follows: "The inner search for the lost object is the vital force behind creative conceptualization. It is used as an initial step for creative activity . . . The release of those free-floating fantasy supplies of primary-process thinking for secondary-process pursuits seems to demand a temporary break with the object world" (p. 173). Hauser (1958), commenting on the writings of Proust, has expressed the same thought as follows: "The artist's way to his work leads to a loss of reality, and his way back to reality is a result of his work."

To put it in a nutshell, the ability to form a creative illusion as an emotional reality is the ability to let go of current real objects and by way of regression to discover the connection to the earlier internalized object; to create an illusion on the basis of the infant's transitional experience, at first with the inner object; and later to transfer it by the means and methods of the adult ego to such an external actuality as makes it possible for others to partake of the experience. For this reason an autistic experience or a distinctly narcissistic performance cannot attract the audience as a creative experience does, but instead will elicit feelings of strangeness and even fear, as for instance schizophrenic manifestations very often do.

Creativity that originates in the early experiences of the mother-child relationship is, therefore, a highly developed form of reciprocal oral eroticism *lacking the emotion of envy,* and having instead the feeling of unity. This type of creativity contains the desire to take and to give within the boundaries of the shared creative illusion. When we appraise a work of art, when we read a poem, or when we inspect a piece of work that arouses our feeling of creativity, our experience is of receiving, deeply and strongly, something impressive that we wish to share with someone by describing the experience to him. No trace of envy is present. We have received the creative illusion by identifying with the creative giver and through regression. The illusion has been conjured up for us with the aid of the inner object of the creative artist.

The primary internalized object is the mother or mother substitute, and in view of the development of creativity, the infant has not only integrated his own emotions toward or his experiences of the mother, he has also internalized a part of the mother's adult features, her so-called "inner space" features (see Chapter 4), by identifying with her and by preoccupying himself with her "inner space." It seems to me that the creative illusion of the transitional phase is, at first, more the product of the child's own fantasy, although later on it can be the creative illusion offered by the mother or someone else in the form of a fairy tale or the like. The child experiences only a minimum of envy if he can identify with the mother and internalize her inner space features, whereas mother envy is present and is intensified when the child is unable to enjoy creative companionship and must resort to various means in order to defend himself against envy.

FROM MOURNING TO CREATIVITY

Creativity and mourning have a common denominator in that, in both, libido is withdrawn from the current object. This withdrawal takes place in creativity as the result of regression, and in mourning as the result of object loss. By means of the creative process something new is fashioned, something that can be shared with another. As a result of the mourning process the object is totally lost, and libido must find a new object. In both processes libidinal cathexis is shifted from its fixed position, and the result is a new libidinal constellation. The processes, however, are dissimilar, and in my opinion they are not parallel with but *contiguous* to each other. Whenever grief over loss or mourning is interrupted or has ended, creativity can take the function of a more thorough process of working through without the need for ego defense mechanisms or other functions that would cut off the process. It is also possible to dream or to experience a shared creative illusion with the already lost and mourned object. Mourning is a process that molds a person's object cathexes and integrations, leading to adaptation to changed circumstances, whereas creativity is not merely an adaptive process, but a process that brings with it a new and enriching element, drawing its energy from the narcissistic and object-libidinal cathexis. In this sense, mourning and creativity *complement* each other in the working through of loss. Loss and the ensuing mourning work can lead to quite good adaptation; nevertheless, it does not wipe out the object libido that has existed.

Total disappearance of the object in the emotional sense, its nonexistence outside our range of comprehension, and memories of the lost object relation are always ready for revival, although they no longer contain sorrowful longing. Especially when an adult loses an object of the genital level — a child or spouse — that has also been narcissistically very significant, and equally when a child loses a parent, the mourn-

ing process may be interrupted because a narcissistic offense
has been experienced. Even fully accomplished mourning
work may still require additional working through, inner
reorganization, and creative expression in order to make
possible the acquisition of narcissistic equilibrium. This process is dissimilar to pathological mourning work, with its
depressive and ambivalent features. Creative regression and
creativity lead to the connecting point of primary narcissism
and object libido in the form of the shared illusion of the
mother-child relationship of the child's transitional phase.
When this is the foundation for the creative illusion, creative
regression generally leads to such an intense unity and mutual
understanding in creativity that the shaken libidinal equilibrium is stabilized. Thus the feeling of intimacy and unity
awakened in the transitional phase becomes a safeguard when
later in life object losses tend to frustrate these emotions, as is
the case when one loses a beloved family member. Creativity is
then a part of that integration and adaptation to which the loss
has led.

An adult woman in analysis working through her losses
described her mourning work as it continued in creative
activity as follows: During analysis she had worked through the
loss of her father, which had occurred during her adolescence.
Piece by piece she had gone through memories and personal
characteristics of her father. She had worked through some of
them in the transference experiences, and her libidinal attachment had been transferred elsewhere. I felt that mourning
work, with the identification with parts of the lost object and
the integration of changes caused by the loss, had already been
accomplished. The analysand, however, felt that something
was amiss, and she was bewildered by the fact that the father
image, earlier so idealized, was now gone and that there was
nothing to replace him. An intense creative spirit, with
accompanying feelings of joy and unity with me, then took
hold of her. She compared herself with the "Mother of Lem-

minkäinen" of the Kalevala, who, having lost her son and being unable to find him anywhere, finally gathered his pieces from the River Tuonela and put them together to make a whole living being. In a way hitherto unknown to her, she now gathered memories and facts about her father, making him whole, forming an inner object who became alive and who gave her the feeling of inner wealth. In her creative activities she used both verbal methods and the methods of a painter.

The created inner picture described here can be expressed by more or less artistic means of creativity, but it never fails to bring forth something new and reviving to replace what has been lost. It is not a compensatory process, since the created object can in no way replace the lost object, nor is it a reorganization of inner structure. I think it has to do with the human inability to experience and to understand that an object so indispensable can totally vanish. The loss can be accepted as the loss of a gratifying object, but the object is created over and over again as an inner illusion or as transformed products of creativity of the external world. This is to be seen most clearly in the manifestations of artistic work, as it can be perceived in the inner personal need to do specific creative work.

Besides being a continuation of mourning in the foregoing manner, creativity can also *take the place of mourning.* Creativity then functions as an ideology, and takes the place of the lost human relationship. The person who has suffered the loss keeps repeating a certain series of thoughts and experiences that are connected with the lost object. Thus an artist, for instance, may manifest compulsive methods in his work — a mannerism — or a scientist may strive in his research for certain reassuring results in order to confirm that the bond to the lost object is still intact. Creative work thus becomes a means of evading painful mourning, which would lead to a final loss of the object, by recreating it in another form. Here the analogy comes to mind of parents who give a dead child's name to the newborn in order to insure the fantasy of life continuing in the second child, who also is their product. The loss, the death of the first child, is thus symbolically mitigated. When creativity takes the form of an ideology, the loss has not been integrated as part of the personality structure; only some features of the object have been internalized and identified with, and they are then repeated. Freud (1917) pointed to the fact that an ideology can replace a lost object relation or take its role, and only when the ideology loses its value can mourning work begin.

The loss of both the familiar object and the accustomed gratification provided by the object arouses feelings of painful longing. Drive gratification has its own customary pattern that has been established as a satisfactory one, and both narcissistic and object-libidinal attachments function smoothly as long as the object remains unchanged. Every change in the nature of the object disrupts drive gratification. In contrast, creativity has an opposite quality, and the discovery of new forms elicits pleasurable feelings. Creativity too contains the element of longing, although it is directed not at old, lost objects, but instead at new experiences heretofore unknown.

The new, created objects and experiences first arise in the form of creative illusion. As far as I can see, the regression of the creative process is first reflected in a longing for the mother-child relationship of the transitional phase, although the object of longing is not the mother or mother symbol as such, as is known to be the case in the problems of alcoholics. The object is the mutual illusion of the transitional phase to form a basis for progressive creative activity, and the created product, like the transitional object, is invested with narcissistic and object libido. The integrated mother-child relationship of the transitional phase provides the ability to form a creative illusion. The mother has the ability to bear offspring, to transfer her narcissistic libidinal devotion cathected in the child to object libido directed at the child, and, on account of woman's creative inner space features, to repeatedly bring forth creative illusions together with the child. This ability is used by creative people as well, and thus creativity and child-bearing have so many common features. It is well known that artistically and scientifically active, creative work and "giving birth" to creative illusions are much more common among men than women. It is possible that a woman can obtain more satisfaction from her biologically creative ability in the form of generativity than can a man.

CREATIVITY AS A SOLUTION FOR MOTHER ENVY

Greenacre (1960), as well as Erikson (1968) and Winnicott (1971), have emphasized the significance of bisexual identifications in active creativity. The basic mode of creativity conforms to woman's biological creative potential to produce offspring. The course creativity takes could be defined as inspiration, expansion and elaboration of the idea in the mind, and transposition of the idea into external form. Correspondingly, producing a child consists of impregnation, pregnancy, and delivery. Creativity is probably the only means the male has of identifying with the child-producing mother, his creative mind taking on the function of "woman's inner space." This train of thought is reflected in fairy tales and in mythology, as for instance in the ancient Greek myth of Zeus giving birth to Pallas Athene from his head. In this sense creativity affords a person, regardless of age and sex, the chance to identify with motherhood and to experience in creativity the intimate unity of the mother-child relationship and the creative illusion of the transitional phase.

Creativity must not, however, be regarded as a compensatory mechanism born to defend the ego against mother envy, like phallic defense (see Chapter 4). On the contrary, its basis is identification with motherhood and the internalization of it, and therefore its basic pattern is one of growth and development. This point of view facilitates understanding the significance of creativity in loss and mourning: creativity offers the experience of unity in the empty external world of grief, as it also makes possible the production of something new to enrich both inner and outer existence after the loss has been worked through as an inner experience.

On the basis of psychoanalytic observation, Jacobson (1950) considers that a boy cherishes the wish to bear children, and that, for instance, there are men, often of creative personality, whose feminine qualities are fixated to the jealousy they feel toward pregnant and childbearing women. She proposes that creative work and creativity normally could offer the male an opportunity, by way of sublimation, to realize his desire to bear a child. Van der Leeuw (1958) has presented a corresponding view of man's reactions, in the light of psychoanalytic cases, when the male accepts the fact that he is unable to become pregnant and to bear a child like the mother. He says: "The obstacles to be overcome are the feelings of rage, jealousy, rivalry, and above all of impotence and helplessness, and the destructive aggression which accompany these experiences. Childbearing is experienced as achievement, power and competition with the mother. It is an identification with the active, producing mother" (p. 115). I believe that this type of mother envy or, on the other hand, identification with an actively child-producing mother in sublimated form, springs from the child's preoedipal desires at a time when he still enjoyed the intense two-person relationship with the mother. In this case, the point is not the desire to take the mother's place as the father's sexual partner in accordance with the fantasies of the oedipal phase, which is the identification pattern of male homosexuality; rather, it is the identification with the mother in the interaction of the two-person relationship. It is probable, however, that when only slightly sublimated, preoedipal identification with the mother can lead to oedipal identification with her as the father's sexual partner instead of to identification with her inner space features.

A child's desires, his envy, his rage, as well as his identification, are in themselves unconscious processes to the child himself and to the adult, and only the reactions, the symptoms, and the sublimation leading to creativity are perceptible on the psychosocial level.

PHALLIC ILLUSION AND PHALLIC CREATIVITY

Phallic illusion as a defense against castration anxiety contains the desire of self to be big, strong, handsome, admired, and superior to others, or the desire to be the object of these qualities. The phallic ethos has an active as well as a passive side: power, strength, and honor—submission, self-sacrifice, and reverence. Phallic illusion possesses a quality of creativeness unlike that based on Winnicott's transitional phase of the mother-child relationship, and on the inner space features of the mother (see Chapter 4). Phallic illusion is an *entirely narcissistic* experience. The person himself is the object of his own libidinal emotions, and he wishes to be the object of the libido of others without interacting with them. In its passive form, phallic illusion means that the person is the admirer, the servant, or the muse of an object invested with phallic qualities or phallic fantasies. Thus there is no joy, no liberating emotion of mutual association and understanding, in the phallic creative experience, but on the contrary a binding and imprisoning assessment and a restriction of oneself for the attainment of a fixed goal.

A phallic creative person builds around himself. The created product stands or falls with him, and it may be grasped by others only because its maker is renowned. On the other hand, phallic creativity can lean on common phallic symbols, symbols of might that are connected with the per-

sonality of a known individual. *Phallic creativity* is characteristic of rulers, of power seekers, and of those in pursuit of
submission to the protection of the phallic sword. A most
distinctive example of this can be found in the magnificent
pyramids of ancient Egypt. The opposite is the spirit of
creativity in folk tradition, which has an epic quality, reveals
and unites, and with which anyone can identify in a creative
way. This kind of creativity is to be found in a people's
traditional customs of working and feasting, as well as in their
expressive folklore.

Phallic illusion imitates the creative illusion of inner space,
and the phallic organization is erected as a defense against the
child's envy of the mother's inner space. In this sense, phallic
creativity is an attempt to abolish not only castration anxiety
but separation anxiety as well. The phallicly creative person is
able to experience that he is not alone, has not been abandoned and is not worthless, when he inspects himself and his
own narcissistic value in the emotional reactions of those
around him. Separation anxiety, however, is not eliminated by
phallic creativity as it is by inner space creativity, or the
creativity of a folk tradition, in a way that joins people
together, except when a group strives toward a common
narcissistically creative goal. Such a goal, for example, is the
emphasized conception of the superiority of a race, of a group
of people.

Phallic illusion and phallic creativity in the grief of loss and
in mourning are not an extension or a part of mourning, but
rather a means of *defense against loss* in a way that enhances
the person's phallic-narcissistic value. By means of the phallic
defensive organization and phallic creativity, the person tries
to rise above the narcissistic wound caused by the loss and the
defeat. There is no experience of grief in this event, for the
emotion has been averted, and its place has been taken by
triumph and heightened self-esteem. It is apparent that
experiencing grief, working through mourning, and attaining

actual creativity cannot begin until the phallic defense has sufficiently subsided. This is to be perceived, for instance, in the poetry of Edith Södergran during the mourning process when she awaited approaching death (see Chapter 2).

As a brief summary, it can be stated that creativity has a profound significance in grief and in mourning in the internalization of and adaptation to the process, although in two opposing ways. Phallic-narcissistic creativity is a part of phallic defense organization, and thus has the quality of defensively parrying loss and halting the mourning process. Creativity that has sprung from the child's transitional phase and from the mother's inner space features, and that has been sublimated and developed, contributes to the mourning process in a way that enriches the personality and brings people together.

PART III

A Study of Psychotherapy of Three Dying Patients from a Psychoanalytic Viewpoint

6.

The Child's Reactions to Death

A REVIEW OF THE LITERATURE

In the psychic sense the problems involved in the dying process vary according to the age of the individual. In many respects the process is different for a child, an adolescent, a middle-aged person, and an old person. There are differences in ego structure and emotional dependence on the environment at different ages. An infant is entirely dependent on the ability of one person, the mother or mother substitute, to insure him the possibility of life, both physically and emotionally. A very old person, on the other hand, has emotionally become nearly independent of others, and may with satisfaction live with his memories and inner objects. Response to the loss of a valued object—the mother in childhood, a parent in adolescence, a spouse in adulthood—varied markedly in quantitiy and quality.

REACTIONS TO TOTAL LOSS

The loss that has to be faced in one's own death is a total one, and therefore, regardless of age, it is the same for everyone. Total loss lies outside the sphere of our comprehension, and Freud (1915) expressed the idea as follows: "... in the unconscious every one of us is convinced of his own immortality" (p. 289). An existence without being alive and without objects is inconceivable to human powers of perception, although it can be understood by excluding the impossibilities and accepting the inevitability of death. It is obviously impossible to lose totally, and to decathect all objects by mourning. There is a boundary beyond which are found imperceptiveness and the unconscious faith in life's unending continuity. Studies of dying adults have contained suggestions of this (F. Deutsch, 1935; Sandford, 1957; Joseph, 1962; Norton, 1963; Eissler, 1955; this volume, Chapter 1). In their fear of death the patients resorted to various ego defenses against the total loss, the defenses changing as the process of dying advanced. They turned to fantasies and substitute objects in place of losses, and employed an auxiliary ego against the fear of death. As the dying process advanced and the psychic regression progressed, some of these patients, at the end, experienced a symbiotic union with their mothers, either in the transference to the therapist or in fantasies of life after death.

THE LOSS OF THE MOTHER IN INFANCY

It seems that it is impossible to decathect the object of early infancy, the mother or mother substitute, by mourning as it is later in life when the loss of objects is mourned. The loss of the mother in infancy is an experience too total and too close to the fear of one's own death for the child to be able on his own to perceive it as a final one. When the possibility of totally losing the mother in childhood dawns on one, one denies it and takes refuge in omnipotent fantasies in the same way that one does in adulthood when one denies death as the total loss of objects. Eissler (1955) distinguishes two separate fears of impending death. The first fear is that of being without a future, and it is accompanied by a fear of destruction of the psyche, of the soul, of the ego, or of the personality. The second fear is related to destruction of the body and to annihi-

lation, without necessarily containing the fear of losing personality, and therefore it is less total. These two forms of fear
of death come very close to the sources of anxiety in childhood
(Freud, 1923; Waelder, 1960); the fear of losing the object, the
mother, who gratifies important needs, or later her love and
care; and the fear of castration or maiming of the body.
Winnicott (1960) states that anxiety in these early stages of the
parent-infant relationship relates to the alternatives of being
and annihilation.

> Under favourable conditions the infant establishes a con-
> tinuity of existence and then begins to develop the sophisti-
> cations which make it possible for impingements to be
> gathered into the area of omnipotence. At this stage the
> word death has no possible application, and this makes the
> term death instinct unacceptable in describing the root of
> destructiveness. Death has no meaning until the arrival of
> hate and of the concept of the whole human person. When
> a whole human person can be hated, death has meaning,
> and close on this follows that which can be called maiming;
> the whole hated and loved person is kept alive by being
> castrated or otherwise maimed instead of killed [p. 47].

Obviously fantasies of omnipotence developed in childhood
protect the child against the possibility of destruction of his
personality, while castration or some other maiming or even
destruction of his body represent a more acceptable form of
death.

In the proximity of impending death there is fear, but also
the capacity to be alone. Winnicott writes (1958) that in
addition to the three-body relationship of the Oedipus
complex, and the two-body relationship of the mother and
child, there is also the one-body relationship to solitude. He
points out that "the ability to be truly alone has as its basis the
early experience of being alone in the presence of someone.
Being alone in the presence of someone can take place at a very

early stage, when the ego immaturity is naturally balanced by ego-support from the mother. In the course of time the individual introjects the ego-supportive mother and in this way becomes able to be alone without frequent reference to the mother or mother symbol" (p. 32). According to Winnicott, being alone with someone is ego-relatedness in which at least one is "alone," yet the presence of each is important to the other. This is something other than the id relationship in which gratification of drives is the most important aim. A child's being alone with his mother is ego-relatedness which can also be the matrix of transference. He states that "Maturity and the capacity to be alone implies that the individual has had the chance through good-enough mothering to build up a belief in a benign environment. This belief is built up through a repetition of satisfactory instinctual gratification" (p. 32). It is therefore to be expected that the person confronted with impending death faces separation from familiar objects and the assumed solitude according to the capacity for being alone that he has developed. When this capacity is exceeded he needs the ego support of the external world to be freed from the anxiety of separation. It is obvious that a small child needs more ego support than an older child or an adult to be able to be alone without anxiety.

REACTIONS TO THE DEATH OF A CHILD

The task of mourning related to a child's death contains an important phase of relinquishing existing libidinal ties to parents or parent figures. This relinquishing in the face of approaching death has been preceded during the process of growth by libidinal disengagement from the parents, which is dependent not only on the age of the child but also on the nature and intensity of the child-parent relationship, and the interaction between the child and his parents.

When a child dies the parents lose their child in a traumatic way that not only offends them narcissistically but also evokes the emotions of insufficiency and guilt in them. They deny the child's impending death and the task of mourning unconsciously, and often even consciously in the presence of the child, who then adopts their attitude toward death for fear of otherwise bringing the parents' disapproval on himself.

Nagera (1970) expresses the view that in trying to "spare the child" and in keeping important facts from him the parents actually express their intolerance of their own grief, and therefore forbid the child to mention the "painful event." The statement that a child is not capable of feeling true sorrow is in itself a denial of the child's grief, and a defense against the adult's own separation anxiety.

According to Freud (1917),

> Reality-testing has shown that the loved object no longer exists, and it proceeds to demand that all libido shall be withdrawn from its attachments to that object. . . . people never willingly abandon a libidinal position, not even, indeed, when a substitute is already beckoning to them. . . . Each single one of the memories and expectations in which the libido is bound to the object is brought up and hyper-cathected, and detachment of the libido is accomplished in respect of it. . . . when the work of mourning is completed the ego becomes free and uninhibited again [pp. 244-245].

Freud's description of working through mourning is probably the ideal in favorable circumstances but one that remains unattainable even to most adults.

Parkes (1972) noted in his investigation of the mourning of widows that the occurrence of "phantom husbands," a strong sense of the presence of the dead husband near at hand, is more common among them than the absence of such an experience. A parent's "phantom child" or a child's "phantom parent" is an equally common phenomenon when the mourning work has not been completed.

The Child's Capacity to Mourn

Whether a child's working through of mourning is identical with the mourning of an adult as Freud described it is a subject of controversy. According to Anna Freud (1952), a child attains object constancy at the end of the first year or the beginning of the second year of his development, and after this the newly formed cathexis is of a particular quality. The child does not become attached to a substitute object in the same way as before, although he may accept the care of such an object. Nagera (1970) suggests that "it is only at the point when object constancy has been reached that the nature and quality of the cathexis directed to the object can at least in rudimentary form be compared to the level, nature, and quality of the cathexis directed by the normal adult to his closest objects. . . . It is this cathexis that must be withdrawn from the innumerable memories of the lost object and made available for the recathexis of some new objects" (p. 370).

Among those who have investigated the mourning work of children is Bowlby (1960), who has claimed that mourning similar to that of adults has been observed in a child of six months. Anna Freud (1960, 1967), among others, has considered this doubtful, and contends (1960) that "before . . . the stage of object constancy has been reached, the child's reactions to loss seem to us to be governed by the more primitive and direct dictates of the pleasure-pain principle" (p. 180). According to Furman (1964a), a child has the capacity to mourn the loss of his mother from the age of three and a half to four years, whereas Wolf (1958) estimates the age at 10 to 11 years. Nagera (1970) and Wolfenstein (1965, 1966), for their part, claim that the mourning described by Freud is possible only after separation from the parents in adolescence, although some aspects of mourning are already discernible in childhood.

Factors Affecting the Capacity to Mourn

I agree with Furman (1964a) that observation of a child's mourning should be carried out keeping in mind two different aspects: first, the child's personal capacity to mourn; and second, the factors that inhibit the utilization of that capacity. Furthermore, it is important to distinguish the absence of manifest signs of grief, as well as the child's possible neurosis arising therefrom, from the fact that the child may not have the capacity to mourn. Thereby great individual differences are also made comprehensible; for instance, a four-year-old may be capable of intense mourning, whereas a child in latency may not have the same capacity. In difficult circumstances an adult's capacity to mourn is also diminished. De Wind (1968) has noted that prisoners in extermination camps such as Auschwitz did not mourn, but instead adjusted themselves to the circumstances by means of archaic ego functions.

The child's personal capacity to mourn is affected by the phase of development through which he is passing, and also by his earlier traumatic experiences. The necessary and inevitable frustrations related to optimal development do not hurt a child's healthy omnipotence as do traumatic events. Healthy omnipotence includes the belief that the future will be a good one. Lacking this, the child becomes fixated on or regresses to the security of the past, or to past omnipotent fantasies. Traumas experienced earlier and the absence of constant security lessen the child's ability to mourn his losses. Another element that lessens the child's capacity to mourn is found in existing circumstances at the time of the loss. Nagera (1970) points out that we tend to underestimate the tremendous importance of perceptual and environmental constancy for the human being, especially for the child in bereavement. Familiar surroundings and objects, familiar possessions (room, bed, toys, etc.), familiar noises, are important for our well-being.

He further contends that there is a great difference between the mourning of children placed in institutions, hospitals, and the like, and that of children who remain at home in familiar surroundings in their position as family members. Investigations of children's mourning have mainly concerned children who have been either permanently or temporarily removed from their homes. To quote Anna Freud (1960): "From direct observation we know little or nothing about the duration of grief in those instances where the mother has to leave temporarily or permanently while the child remains at home" (p. 182). It seems that when the relatives are able to give support to the child in expressing and accepting his sorrow, and do not encourage the denial of it, the child is able to accept the loss of a close relative by mourning. Barnes (1964) has presented the case of two little girls, aged two and a half and four, who came to understand the meaning of death and were capable of mourning their mother's death after their relatives had received guidance and therapy that enabled them to support these children. Shambaugh (1961) and Furman (1964b) have described how two children aged six and seven, were supported by analysis to work through intense mourning of their mothers' deaths.

What, then, are the circumstances that obstruct a child's capacity to mourn and cause him to deny the loss in speech, in functions, in fantasies, and in affects? In addition to the factors already mentioned, answers to the following questions must be sought: First, when is a child capable of understanding the external realities related to death, and death itself as an irreversible event? Second, when does a child have the capacity to undertake the painful and agonizing process involved in the decathecting of a beloved and significant person that is so indispensable to the task of mourning? In "Absence of Grief" Helene Deutsch (1937) pointed to the phenomenon of indifference that children so often display after the death of a loved person. Wolfenstein (1965) has also noted that before adolescence children are not capable of enduring protracted mourning like adults. Nagera (1970) points to similar experiences, but suggests that "much of the behavior of the adult world under bereavement conditions is a conventional and generally accepted, ritualized type of behavior. This makes little sense to the young child who has not yet come across it and has not introjected it as the appropriate code of behavior under such circumstances" (p. 372, fn. 7).

For several years I have observed the reactions of three children, aged five, seven, and 11, to the death of their mother. With the support of adults they were able to express their painful sorrow verbally and affectively, as well as by expressing their fantasies of the mother's approaching death when the end was near. After her death they dwelt on memories of her, showing great longing. Somewhat later they improvised a song of an "old, skinny cow" to be sung together, while perceiving the reference to their mother who was now worthless and dead. They have cherished innumerable memories of their mother, and have been able to grow attached to their stepmother with no sign of a splitting of feelings or of idealization of either one. I believe that if the family culture supports and maintains mutual sorrow and mutual joy, then, owing to ego support, the children are able to endure the pain related to hypercathexis or decathexis of the lost object.

THE CHILD'S ABILITY TO MASTER THE CONCEPT OF DEATH

Furman (1964a) contends that

Applied to the ability to master the concept of death, the necessary levels of reality-principle acceptance and of reality testing would require: (1) sufficiently stable and differentiated self and object representations in the inner world so that the integrity of the self representation can withstand the threat implicit in the death of someone else; (2) sufficient ego mastery over the id so that the concept of death can be relatively more integrated within the ego's expanding pool of knowledge rather than utilized for the arousal of instinctual derivatives; (3) the ability to distinguish animate from inanimate and thus have a concept of the living as opposed to the nonliving; (4) some ability to understand time in terms of the past, present, and future; and (5) sufficient secondary-process causal thinking to understand that since something is dead, it can no longer do certain things [p. 325].

Furman believes that these ego functions have reached maturity at the age of two to three years so that the child is capable of understanding the meaning of death.

It is probably more common, however, for a child to deny the irreversibility of death with fantasies of the dead person returning, or living in heaven, etc. Anna Freud and Burlingham (1944) have cited many examples of this procedure, assuming that the mother has sometimes influenced it through her efforts to spare the child pain by withholding the truth, and that it has sometimes been the spontaneous production of the child himself. I have observed a child of three who unexpectedly found his little dog dead. He looked at it, touched it, and decided that it was dead, and should be thrown into the trash can. Even when he was longing for his dog later he did not express the idea that the dog could be somewhere, and that it might return, but seemed to understand the finality of death. Nagera (1970) has indicated by references to the literature how the age-adequate thought processes of a child influence his reactions to and understanding of death: "He obviously makes efforts to understand the painful events on the basis of his previous knowledge. It is not his fault if the adult world feeds him a great deal of distorted and misleading information. His attempts at mastery can only be based on that information. On the other hand, his needs and wishes may at times distort and override factual knowledge . . ." (pp. 378-379).

Discussing death with a child is a very difficult task for an adult, because he must then reveal his own futility, limitations, and insecurity to the child. Furthermore, a discussion of death with a child is more suggestive of oedipal competition and the death wishes of the rival than is a discussion between adults. Anna Freud (quoted by Nagera, 1970), commenting on the subject, believes that "adults frequently try to keep contact with death away from the child at a time when he is interested in and can approach the subject . . . By doing so one surrounds death in mystery, as a dark and secret subject not to be puzzled out and understood" (p. 379, fn. 10). She believes that "adults . . . are really protecting themselves from the child's sadism" by evading the issue when the child in the anal-sadistic phase approaches injury and death not with horror but with fascination. There are many reasons for an adult to surround death in mystery, to keep it a dark and secret subject. One reason may be the same as the reason for adult secretiveness about sex: the underlying aim is to control the younger generation, spurred by the fear that if children are enlightened about such matters, they will control the adults.

CLINICAL ILLUSTRATION: A 12-YEAR-OLD BOY'S REACTIONS TO HIS OWN DEATH

ONSET OF THE ILLNESS

I call my patient Tom. When it became evident that Tom was afflicted with acute leukemia, he was 10 years old. At the time he was an inpatient in a children's hospital because of pains in his back that had begun after a fall in the schoolyard a month earlier. The patient died at the age of 12 years and two months, two years and one month after the disease was detected.

When Tom was admitted to the hospital after the first relapse with leukemia, his conduct toward the staff and other patients was aggressively offensive. He threatened to stab them with scissors and knives. I was therefore called in, as the hospital psychotherapist, and after a consultation it was decided that I should take the patient into psychotherapy. I then continued to see the patient two or three times a week, an hour at a time, during the periods of hospitalization until his death.

THE PATIENT'S BACKGROUND

Tom was the first-born in the family. The relationship between his parents was shaded by various conflicts. Tom's father was quite a heavy drinker, and his mother indulged in extramarital affairs. Tom had a brother, a year younger than himself, whom the father, however, did not acknowledge as his son. From early infancy Tom had been mostly taken care of by his paternal grandmother. When he was four years old he and his father moved away to another neighborhood. The parents were then divorced, and the father soon remarried. Thereafter Tom never saw his own mother again. After the father's second marriage Tom saw less of his grandmother because mother-in-law and new daughter-in-law did not get on very well. The father's second marriage turned out very well, and he practically stopped drinking.

Tom and his stepmother were very much attached to each other. She came to see him in the hospital quite often, except near the end. Sometimes she brought along Tom's little three-year-old half sister, of whom the boy was very fond and whose visits he eagerly anticipated. For the most part the boy's father saw his son only on his short visits at home. The father represented an authority for Tom, someone to admire from a distance. They had a mutual hobby in playing chess, and the game offered an important means of contact between them.

Both parents had jobs in the same shop. They felt financially secure. The father was an atheist, whereas the mother's attitude to religion was one of indifference. The boy had been offered no fantasies at home about life continuing in a different form after death; rather, he had been told that death is the end of everything. Discussions about death had taken place two years earlier, on the occasion of the step-mother's father's death and burial.

Tom's falling ill with leukemia took his parents unawares; for his father especially it was a shock. He reacted by saying that he could not understand it and could do nothing about it, and by withdrawing. The mother had shown signs of sorrow in the early phase of Tom's illness, but toward the end she too withdrew. At the very beginning the parents had been informed of the nature of Tom's disease, and that he would live two years at the most. Tom himself had been told at first that he suffered from an ailment in his back, and that he would recover. Not until he had the second relapse was he told that he really suffered from a blood disease. When Tom asked his mother if he was going to die, she answered that everyone does in due time, and the boy left it at that.

PSYCHOTHERAPY

It was possible to carry on psychotherapy only during the periods of hospitalization, because Tom's parents could not bring him to therapy from home nor did they allow him to come alone. They did not wish me to come to their home to see Tom either. Therapy was therefore divided into three parts, and the total duration was one year and three months.

Phase I: Transference to the Therapist Taking Shape

To begin with, Tom declared that he was very bored in the hospital. He did not wish to mix with other patients, but

instead retreated to his own room. He found a boy called Ari
very annoying—he knew the boy suffered from the same blood
disease as he himself. Tom had threatened to stab Ari with a
pocketknife if he came into his room. Tom accepted the
therapy agreement with joy, and showed eagerness for the
contact, but at the same time he was on his guard. He wanted
to know why I came to see him. I told him I liked to come, and
that he might find my visits useful, without making any
reference to his illness or to the conflicts on the ward.

Tom told me that he had to take great care when walking
lest he fell and hurt his back, and for this reason he mustn't go
out. He felt it was a good arrangement for me to come to see
him, because he might forget the time agreed on for therapy.
While talking he modeled a human figure from plasticine, and
at his request I modeled a boat. He put the boat into water and
gradually loaded it until it sank. He continued doing this for a
long time, and described the various articles the boat could
carry.

During the next therapy sessions he modeled cars and
drivers. He was very careful not to make a mess, and kept
cleaning up scraps. He told me that he was afraid of slipping
and hurting his back accidentally, and that traffic was very
dangerous. He told me about a nightmare he had had just
before becoming ill, describing how, in the dream, he was in
the war and was shot. He had sensed that he was falling dead
and, waking up at the same time, he found himself falling off
his bed. He pondered over the possibility of having already
hurt his back then.

Tom began to express his various fears more and more
clearly. He drew pictures of a boy on paper, but only of the
head, remarking, "The rest isn't important," and pointing out
that the face had a frightened expression. He described how
frightened he was of being struck by a car in traffic, and how
bad it felt when someone came up from behind and put hands
over his eyes, asking in a gruff voice, "Guess who's here?" He

was afraid of looking at TV news — he was afraid of Arab guerrillas coming to Finland — of increasing industrial smoke poisoning the air, and of no one being able to live without a gas mask at the end of the century. He also felt sad because his stepmother came to see him less often than before.

Tom's strong efforts to control and curb his feelings weakened little by little, and he was annoyed because he was not allowed to go home. He no longer tried to understand this, but aimed his anger at the doctors attending him. He was angry, and yet his mind was filled with abundant fantasies of life on another planet. He told me about the possibility of there being life on other planets. He tried to imagine the appearance of the people living there, and to draw them in comic-strip fashion. He was not satisfied with his drawing nor did he try to do it again, but instead expressed himself by telling stories about them. He thought that the language on the other planet might be quite the opposite of ours, and that he would understand it by reading the words backwards. Besides their appearance and language, he also thought about the people's age. He explained that time passes at a different tempo on another planet, that a 50-year-old there might be 40 years younger than here, and therefore a son could be the same age as his father. This imaginative play was a source of great satisfaction to him. He became really boisterous, and excitedly described how an atomic bomb bigger than the Hiroshima one would destroy Finland and the Finnish people. At the same time consciousness of his own physical weakness bothered him more and more, and while expounding his aggressive fantasies he took care that he had a pillow behind his back and on each side, and even told me to exchange the frail-looking chair on which I was sitting for a more solid one.

Tom then told me that he had the same blood disease as Ari, and that he therefore got strong drugs which made his hair fall out. At the time he was nearly bald, his back was bent and stiff, but he could still walk without help. He was some-

what downhearted and quiet, and said he didn't feel well
because he was so ill. He had been making a paper creature
with a huge mouth that he called "Ellu," meaning Elmer, a
comic-strip hero. (Elmer is a little, bald, busy, and industrious
man pestered by Daffy and Bugs Bunny, two harmful teases
whom he tries to get rid of, finding himself constantly losing
the battle.) While Tom was talking he held Ellu in his hand
and spoke to me through Ellu's mouth, showing great affection
for me. He started to fly airplanes that were dropping bombs
on us, and we had to take shelter. Then, without a word, he
began to feed Ellu with bombs, and when I verbalized this to
him he seemed amused. He then made Ellu vomit, and then
fed him again, doing this by turns, and finally, making him a
cigarette, he said that now Ellu would fall ill with lung cancer
and die. He then gave Ellu to me for keeps, saying, "Maybe
you will see something in it."

Tom spent Sunday at home, and after that he was quiet
and only wanted to play chess. He said he had played chess
with his father during his stay at home too. After that weekend
I saw Tom twice, and then his parents took him home
unexpectedly, without giving me the opportunity to prepare
him for the separation. The stepmother told me she could not
resist the boy's pleading now that he felt better.

Phase II: Resorting to Magic-Omnipotent Fantasies

When Tom was at home alone in the daytime, he had told
his parents that he wanted to see me. His teacher had called
every day, and Tom had made good progress in his studies,
having been granted a scholarship at his school. When he
came to the outpatient clinic after an interim of two months,
he told me that it had been very difficult to cross the street
because of street repairs, and he had had to take a long route
in order to cross over. He wondered if I was annoyed by street
repairs and workers, and said he felt bad about the street being
torn up by excavation. He told me about wanting to phone me

earlier, but his parents had said that he could see me when he came to have his blood tests taken at the hospital. Then he mentioned having seen a spider in my room on his first visit. He had been afraid of it then, but now it was gone. He told me that he had seen the TV program in which I was interviewed about the attitude toward a dying person. He said he had liked the program. He inspected my room and its various objects carefully, asking me very personal questions, as if he were searching for something. After his return home the same evening he had become restless, and complained that his back hurt. The next day he was admitted to the hospital again.

When I entered his room that day, Tom bade me a cheerful welcome. He told me how thunder clouds had hovered in the sky for many days, and while he was saying this there was a distinct rumble of thunder. Tom was scared and said, "I believe I said the magic words."

During the following therapy hours he had many fantasies about possessing supernatural powers, and about how different everything would then be. These fantasies were especially connected with visual powers—seeing an airplane through the ceiling, seeing what I was doing when I was not in his company. He made a talisman of fur and cardboard for himself, and felt that it gave him protection hanging on the wall above his bed. He then made a great many more of them, dwarflike things, and sold them to members of the staff. When they kindly showed interest and bought them, he reacted by jeering and despising them, and wondered if they were really serious about his amulets.

Tom's ability to move had conspicuously deteriorated, and he could walk only by making a great effort. He leaned more often on me or members of the staff for help. Various games became important to him now, especially a game called African Star. The winner was the one who found the biggest diamond. He mentioned that he had a financial game in store, a game to be played for as long as two years, a nice way to pass the time in a bomb shelter, for example. He never suggested that we should play this game, however. While we were playing African Star, Tom described the dream he had had the night before: he had been in an undertaker's cellar, where there were many bodies and coffins. He had been shut in, and the door was locked. He was afraid, and through the door could hear gangsters saying that he would be hanged. Then a secret agent came and rescued him. There was a fight and a general commotion, and he woke up. It had been a nightmare, and on waking he felt he had been saved from evil, which was a great relief to him. After this he became absorbed in a fantasy game of the two of us going to the moon to fetch moon stones. Fantasy was interwoven with fear and anxiety, and when the game was over Tom felt relieved and said, "Now we have been to the moon, and are back again."

Before the next interruption of therapy, caused by my one-month vacation, Tom clearly showed conscious feelings of loneliness and of missing me. He told me stories about villains and policemen, and about his own fantasies of them. He especially pondered over the ways a murderer hides the body, and came to the conclusion that it cannot be done successfully. The body is always found. While he wanted to think that murderers are always punished, he felt it very important that the body cannot be completely hidden or destroyed. "It is always found," he thought.

Phase III: The Death Process Reflected in the Transference

Tom had been at home during the pause in therapy, but now returned to the hospital because of a recurrence of his illness. His first words to me were filled with disappointment because I had not called him during my vacation. He was very anxious and frightened. He had had repeated nightmares of gangsters threatening to kill him. But he always got away, and on waking was relieved to find that he had escaped from the peril. He did not dare get out of bed any longer because he was

afraid of stumbling. His fears had now come closer to conscious fear of death. He told me that he had confidence in the
doctors caring for him and in me, but at the same time he felt
uncertain because I might not be able to wake him from his
sleep when I came to see him. He was often fast asleep on my
arrival. The fear of "falling asleep forever" was also manifested
in fear of losing his memory and of not recognizing himself any
more on waking. He tried to find an object for fear outside
himself. From his window he showed me a construction crane
that he kept watching, afraid it might fall over on somebody.
Every time he awoke he was relieved to find the crane still
there. He began asking questions about what was done in the
hospital when somebody died, wanting to make sure that the
family was informed. Truthful information set his mind at
peace, especially the knowledge that no one is left alone to die.

Having these matters straightened out in his mind, and
being totally dependent on the help of nurses in getting to a
sitting position or into the wheel chair, Tom became fretful
and faultfinding. He talked about war, about men's wish to
destroy one another, and about the uncertainty of the world at
large. Once again he started to develop fantasies about the
moon. He pictured it as a forlorn, lonely place without any
vegetation, but thought that plastic houses and flowers might
decorate it. He also believed that the time for regular moon
flights was near. The anger he now felt toward nurses and
doctors was manifested in accusations and crankiness, and also
in imagining that nurses could kill their patients by admin-
istering the wrong medicine. "Patients were entirely helpless in
their hands," he thought. Tom's hatred of nurses reached its
peak during a blood transfusion, but afterwards he felt strong
guilt at having vented his emotions and was afraid of being
abandoned for his conduct.

Suddenly Tom's mood changed, and he began to arrange a
stamp collection. He was obviously pleased when the staff
started to bring him heaps of stamps, and he made a point of it

that they were valuable gifts. He became much attached to his stamp collection, took great care in arranging it, and believed it was very valuable. He was content now that he had something to do for a long time ahead, and said that "his collection would keep its value at least a hundred years." I was not allowed to touch his stamps lest they be torn. Later on he bequeathed his stamp collection to his parents. Collecting stamps and our chess games were very important to him for several months. At that time his behavior toward the staff was one of superiority, like a diva giving them orders. I was his comrade and friend in games and leisure. His libidinal interest lay in collecting stamps, but in a game of chess he fought in earnest.

The peace of mind he had achieved was badly shaken by the news of a spinal-fluid test to be made. When he heard about it he shouted angrily and tied an electric cord tightly around his neck, threatening to hang himself. The doctors then canceled the test, and the patient felt he had frightened them off. When I entered his room he had a candle burning on his night table. He told me it was a dynamite stick, and he was a dynamite man, and, if he wanted to, he could blow the whole hospital into thin air. His fear of the spinal-fluid test was connected not so much with the pain involved as with the idea of having his backbone fractured and of consequently dying. In this connection he spoke freely of his fear of death, and said he felt so feeble that he didn't believe he would live very long. This took place about four months before his death.

Tom began to talk freely about his fear of death to other people also. At this point his stepmother considerably reduced her visits. Tom was disappointed with his parents, and called them names. He felt that his mother's catching a cold and his father's having a wisdom tooth pulled were poor excuses for not coming to see him. He persuaded his parents to take him home for the week end, but on his return to the hospital he was filled with despair and disappointment because of their inability to help him. He wept heartbrokenly, and moaned that his parents did not care about him. At this point he turned for protection to a children's nurse in the hospital, who took to sitting by his bedside in the evenings, letting him talk about his fear of death. The boy's parents had disapproved of my visits, and he let me know through the doctor in charge that I should not come to see him any more. However, only two days later my visits were considered indispensable because Tom lay awake at nights, shouted, and spat on people.

When I came again, Tom was on his guard, trying to curb his strong feelings. He turned his back on me and burst in tears. When I told him that his parents wanted me to come to see him, he composed himself.

After this phase, Tom was at times cooperative and at others in opposition. He mourned the loss of his parents, whose virtue he would at times exaggerate, and then again find great fault with them. He applied similar emotions to his own body, exaggerating either his ability to move or his complete physical misery. Fantasies of the moon once more became important to him after his father gave him stereoscopic slides of the moon. Loss and fantasies of separation were discussed with me and the children's nurse. When he was alone the stamp collection took up his time. Other people had lost their significance for him now. His manner toward them was one of ordinary friendliness.

About a month before his death, having spent a sleepless night in great back pain, Tom met me with rage. Weeping and shouting, he blamed me for not helping him, but instead making him worse. He threw every object he could reach at me, including a glassful of juice in my face. He told me to go home, and to stop prying into his affairs. When I told him that he was angry with me because he could trust me not to leave him, and because I knew how severe his pains were, he started to sob quietly, and after a while fell asleep. There now began a phase in which he greeted me with the accusation that I came only because I was curious about him; "You can't help me so you'd better go home." After these outbursts of anger Tom became trusting again, and enjoyed my company. Sometimes he wept because he felt his strength ebbing, and complained that he could not live much longer. Toward the end he told me repeatedly that he didn't want to see me. I replied that I would come anyway to see how he was. His manner toward the children's nurse who came to see him in the evenings was very much the same. Tom told her about his disappointment in me, and about my inability to help him get well, but he never said a word about her to me.

I told Tom that after five weeks I would go on a trip. When he heard this he began to weep quietly, but after a while he told me about the picture hanging on the wall beside his bed. He and the hospital occupational therapist had made it together. The picture, made in cross-stitch, showed a redbreast bending over its nest. He said he found it very difficult to decide to whom to give the picture. He made no suggestions, but I got the impression that he was expecting me to decide, and I felt a strong desire to have the picture myself. I did not tell this to the patient. When I came to see him again, he told me he had offered the picture to his mother but had been bitterly disappointed because she did not want to have it. At that time the patient was very quiet in my company; he would lie on his bed without uttering a word, looking at me or out of his window. He had told members of the staff about my coming trip, making clear how many details he knew about it. On May 1 Tom arranged a lottery on the ward, with the redbreast picture he had made as a prize. He told me with great satisfaction how much money he had earned by the lottery, how valuable he considered the picture to be, and how everybody thought so.

Shortly after that Tom contracted pneumonia, and after about a week he died. During this time he was aware of the nearness of death. For instance, he said good-by to a nurse who was going away on her vacation, saying he would not be alive when she came back. Tom's mournful and submissive mood changed when Ari in the next room was dying. Before the end Ari moaned in pain, and in horror Tom banged on the wall with his fist, shouting to Ari to be quiet. Tom had often made comparisons between the developments in their illnesses, wondering which one would live longer. On his last days Tom wanted the children's nurse or his mother to sit by his bedside holding his hand while he lay quietly in bed. When I came to see him he told me he had waited for me, and wanted me to sit by his bedside too. He was not anxious or afraid, but he complained of weakness and fatigue, and he died in his sleep.

SUMMARY OF THE CASE

The case concerned a boy at the end of the latency age. The only constant object relation he had from early infancy was his father. From a very early age he had had two caring mother figures, his own mother and the paternal grandmother. The latter had offered him more security. He lost both during the oedipal period, when his father married again and they both moved to live with his stepmother. He became closely attached to her, and experienced the relationship between his parents as a good one. The traumatic experience of losing both mother and grandmother nevertheless led to a good final outcome when the boy realized that the adult world had become more balanced because conflicts in the home had diminished and the interaction between family members was now based on security. The loss and the fear, and (despite everything) the good final outcome had apparently reinforced his "healthy omnipotence," permitting him the belief that, come what might, all would turn out well in the end. This was reflected in his attitude toward losses as the dying process advanced. No information is available about the ways in which the boy solved the oedipal conflict and its adherent fears, and his libidinal devotion to both sexes. The realistic proximity of death shrouds the neurotic aspect of the problem, and the resolutions of the oedipal conflict are perhaps best seen in the way the patient met his death not only as an inner oedipal conflict but as the loss of his body.

His dreams and fantasies about the disease indicate that he experienced it as an aggressive force from the external world, and in the early stage of the disease he tried to resist it, and to aid recovery in an autoplastic manner by being very obedient, nice, well-mannered. When the first relapse came, he realized that the adults he had trusted had concealed the terrifying truth from him, and he began to defend himself by violent attacks. In the manner befitting latency he tried to change passive suffering and submissiveness to active aggression, and in his fantasies he then became a killer. His wish to stab to death he aimed at other sick children, and especially at the boy with whom he could identify in suffering from the same disease. He wanted to destroy the enemy, the disease, which he saw externalized in another person. This meant identification with the aggressor, an aggressor equivalent to his fantasies of death, so that by destroying the disease in another person he himself would be saved.

At a later stage he tried to change fear of death to more familiar fears: he was afraid of the dangers of traffic, wars, pollution, and so on. When he began to feel angry with the hospital staff caring for him, fantasies about the moon became of interest to him, but these too were frightening and gloomy at this stage. Through these fantasies he tried to make the unknown familiar, and in so doing he could think of life continuing somewhere else; in this respect the fantasies equaled the heaven fantasies of a religious person, although to him they represented only the idea of life's continuance, an idea inherited from his atheist father. The father has had a decisive influence in this respect because he had been the only essentially permanent object, representing the continuity of everything through his views of life. The boy's moon fantasies were indeed bound to the father-son relationship; on the moon they would be the same age. Being the same age as his father would eliminate the oedipal wish, and the danger of dying or of inflicting death on the other. This fantasy lessened the fear of punishment for the boy's own aggressions, and when he became excited he imagined how he would destroy the whole of Finland. He would then not die alone, nor would he lose the constancy of object cathexis represented by his father and his fatherland.

With the weakening of his own physical strength the paper creature, "Ellu," acquired the meaning of an attempt to be freed of the fear of death through a substitute victim. With great satisfaction he forced the substitute to swallow the fatal danger in spite of its attempts to vomit, and finally made it die. The dead substitute he then gave to me as a gift. "Ellu" was the symbol of his weakening body, the symbol of the dying part of himself in relation to which he surrendered his omnipotence, and which he then gave to me. I represented the castrater to him, to whom he gave his body, but the better part, the "soul," he kept himself. After giving me the creature, he manipulated his parents, and the doctor in charge, into allowing him to go home without my knowledge. He then projected his fear of death onto me, and saw lurking death personified in me. On his return to therapy after the interim, he verbalized his magical fear of the fantasies of various objects and a spider he had seen in my room. This fear he tried to curb with fantasies of magical powers in himself; thunder rumbled when he said the magic words; he had the magic eye, and he made a talisman to protect himself. I represented the magician, who in the good sense offered him shelter and help against the fear of death, but in the bad sense I was personified death, to be fended off by fantasies of his own much greater magical powers. Beating me in games meant overcoming death. Every game lost was a source of great anxiety to him for this very reason, and he had the financial game "in store," to be played for as long as two years, thus giving him support by gaining time.

Even though the patient experienced me in his unconscious as personified death, his conscious relation to me at this stage of therapy was one of trust, and there was the sensation of mutual sympathy between us. His dream of murderer-gangster and agent-rescuer depicts the dichotomy already mentioned: he experienced me on the one hand as death, the castrater, and on the other hand as a friend, the rescuer. In the African Star game one returned to the starting point, and the same pattern ruled the game of going to the moon and returning again to earth. Here is the symbol of a mutual journey which does not lead to separation, but to the return of both to the point where the journey was begun. With this fantasy the patient denied the possibility of final separation in relation to my vacation and to his own death. He also denied the possibility of finality regarding the destruction of his own body. Denial as a defense against the fear of separation and annihilation by death was still quite strong at this point.

On his return to the hospital after the second interruption of therapy, he was in very poor physical condition and needed the assistance of others. His fear was akin to conscious fear of death, and he leaned on me with utmost trust, wanting to find out about the outward aspects of death. He directed his distrust and hate at the outside world of the hospital, as well as at the nurses and doctors attending him. At the same time he developed his moon fantasies, which now acquired more warmth in the form of decorative houses and flowers. Omnipotent fantasies of ruling the moon and making changes there became more vivid, while at the same time omnipotent control of his own body was shattered by the progressive physical weakening. The moon became the symbol of a new earth, and a new body. Fear of punishment, or fear of being deserted by the doctors and nurses because of his hatred, now became unbearable, and led to the neutralization of aggression. He became an active stamp collector, inducing others to participate in his hobby and to shower him with gifts. The stamp collection became a very important narcissistic support to him, representing valued and long-lasting life. His narcissism was strengthened by the support of gifts from others. The stamp collection was a good creation of his own, one part of his ego ideal that would continue his life after he had died, and he put it in his parents' possession. The collection reinforced his secondary narcissism, which was a continuation of the narcissism his parents had given him during various phases of his childhood.

When the intimacy and the fear of death had become fully conscious to him, while waiting for spinal-fluid tests he sought protection by using an ultimate means to stay alive. He was afraid of dying of a fractured spine, and as a masochistic defense he threatened to commit suicide. It was not until then that the affects of sorrow, of weakness, and of hatred in mourning work began to dominate. Until then mobilization of libido in mourning work had led to the idealization of important object relations, and to reinforcement of his own narcissism. The latter part of mourning work—the aggressions and the sense of wretchedness—was essentially aimed at his parents. The parents could not face these emotions; their reaction was withdrawal, and disapproval of my visits to the patient. The patient then formed a therapeutic birelation with a children's nurse who had knowledge of and experience in psychotherapy. He worked through the affects of separation from his parents with both of us, but no longer with his parents. The ease with which he formed the transference with the nurse when he was frightened by his parents' reaction was apparently related to the introjection of the mother of infancy, which he had experienced as a sum of many mother figures. In this sense in the transference to the nurse he regressed to the early relationship with his own mother. The growing feebleness of his body and its impending loss he worked through in the same way. In the beginning his sick body was strongly narcissistically cathected. Later he was terrified by the thought that his body might totally vanish, and he worked through that phase. In the end, he sensed the infirmity and worthlessness of his body, and, after mourning, was ready to abandon it. The moon fantasies had not provided the possibility of continuing satisfaction of a real own life, nor did they, in the libidinal and narcissistic sense, replace religious fantasies of a life hereafter. In his last days his ambivalent emotions were completely tied up in present object relations and in the transference to me and the nurse. He aimed primitive emotions of hopelessness, disappointment, and hate at us. Yet during the same therapy hour he was able to show deep devotion and to exhibit sorrow, anxiety, and despair at growing constantly weaker against his will.

News of my coming trip made the patient sad and lowered his self-esteem. He then began to wonder to whom he would give the picture that depicted maternal love. He had internalized the image of a loving mother in his infancy, and the picture symbolized his deepest emotions and the healthy body he was now relinquishing. The picture was his good legacy to another person who would continue to live. The stepmother refused to take the picture, nor did I express my wish to have it. This, I think, is an indication of the universal sense of guilt at showing the dying person that one wants to go on living, while he is losing everything. As an afterthought one feels that the gesture of asking for the picture might have been a source of support and solace to the patient. The patient contracted pneumonia, and a severe regression followed, when he no longer resisted death, but gave up. He sought protection in the presence of another person, and found tranquility in the symbiotic intimacy.

7.

Psychotherapy of Dying Adult Patients

A REVIEW OF THE LITERATURE

Specific Features in Psychotherapy of a Dying Patient

Western culture has tended to isolate death as an alien event, not belonging to the sphere of life. Although death is the end of life, an awareness of death awaiting one in the future is an intrinsic part of living. When the proximity of death becomes an actual fact in the case of illness, and the person is faced with his own death as a reality, the psychic phenomenon is totally different from awareness of the personal end of life as it embraces all mankind. Cappon (1961) has written about the difficulties of facing the problems of a dying patient as follows:

> The surgeon is superstitious. He needs to be optimistic and shuts out twinges of professional guilt and worry. He turns away. The physician feels impotent. Though sympathetic, he turns away. The psychiatrist faces often the threat of man turned against himself; but if suicide is carried through, the psychiatrist also looks away, covered in guilt and shame. Even the priest absorbs his keenest feelings in rituals. The relatives and friends are immersed and

159

blinded by grief, the nurses busy, only the poet and the
philosopher take a look from afar [p. 61].

According to Eissler (1955), the human difficulty in
approaching, dealing with, and working through with the
dying person the problems involved in dying in the intimate
two-person relationship derives, not only from general fear of
death but from the fear of identifying with the dying patient
and of being drawn into the process. Despite the fact that each
and every one in his time must approach death as an actual
experience, the literature contains very few psychologically
and psychodynamically illustrative case reports concerning the
subject. The general reluctance to be emotionally concerned
with dying patients has been frequently referred to by authors
who have presented case reports. They are: Aronsen (1959),
Brodsky (1959), Felix Deutsch (1935), Eissler (1955), Feifel
(1959), Hägglund (this volume, Chapter 1), Joseph (1962),
LeShan and LeShan (1961), Norton (1963), Sandford (1957),
Saul (1959), and Weisman and Hackett (1961). All seem to
share the opinion that there is an imperative need for a
scientific reference system concerning the experiential world of
the dying patient, a need for knowledge and experience of the
transference-countertransference events in the two-person
relationship of a dying patient.

The goal of the psychotherapy of the mentally disturbed
can be said (Rosenthal, 1957) to be "to convert destructive
feelings into constructive, creative self-realization." In the
therapy of the dying patient "the goal is to resolve the negative
feelings toward himself and his past." Thus in the therapy of a
dying patient the past is given more significance than the
future, the scope of which is greatly limited. Fears originating
in the past, feelings of guilt and problems of aggression that
are not directly connected with the proximity of death but are
contained in the death process as neurotic symptoms, must be
differentiated from the actual process. In fact, it has been the

general observation that neurotic symptomatic conflicts can complicate the dying process, and that the sooner they are resolved the less fear of death and anxiety the patient experiences.

Eissler (1955), Rosenthal (1957), and many others have stressed the potential danger of insight therapy to the dying patient. It is not difficult to agree, on the basis of Freud's (1915) observation that "Our unconscious, then, does not believe in its own death; it behaves as if it were immortal" (p. 296). Only the highly developed ego can perceive death as an irreversible phenomenon, but in the deep regression of the dying process, experiencing the death of self as an actual fact is impossible. Although the ego cannot relate to the state of being dead, it experiences the state of having no possibility of drive gratification or object relations as a horrifying one (Eissler, 1955). For this reason the psychotherapy of the patient must conform with each phase according to the depth of the regression reached. The therapy should not break the patient's defense against unbearable anxiety; rather, it should strengthen his ego functions that are still infirm (Hägglund and Hägglund, 1970).

Offering the Transference Relationship to the Dying Patient

A widely adopted viewpoint in the literature of this field is that the dying patient should not be offered ready patterns of dying, nor should any suggestion be made concerning the state after death. Instead, the mechanisms and modes of action that the patient has adopted during various phases of his life, and that correspond to the experiential reality of his regressed state, should be stressed. According to Winnicott (1974), "the clinical fear of breakdown is the fear of breakdown that has already been experienced." He draws attention to the possibility ". . . that the breakdown has already happened, near the beginning of the individual's life. The patient needs to remember this but it is not possible to remember something that has not yet happened to him . . . The only way to 'remember' in this case is for the patient to experience this past thing for the first time in the present, that is to say, in transference." According to Winnicott, "The death, looked at in this way as something that happened to the patient but which the patient was not mature enough to experience, has the meaning of annihilation" (pp. 104, 105).

The decisive meaning of transference in the psychotherapy of a dying patient has been stressed by Norton (1963) and Eissler (1955). The patient's anxiety about dying is decreased when he is able to direct the cathexis withdrawn from objects during mourning work to the therapist in the form of transference fantasies. "Eissler says that the technique of the treatment of the dying patient must center around what he calls 'the gift situation' in which the psychiatrist must create the proper time to make the right gift. The gift is experienced by the patient as 'an unusual . . . favor of destiny'. . . . the really crucial gift the therapist can give is that of himself as an available [transference] object" (Norton, 1963, p. 557).

Norton has described how the transference "allowed [the patient] to externalize her punitive superego and gave her an ego ideal she could live up to . . ." (p. 552). Similarly, Norton (1963) and Eissler (1955) have suggested that the dying patient externalizes his ego onto the therapist in the form of a supportive ego. By the end of the dying process he introjects the therapist (Norton, 1963; Hägglund, this volume, Chapter 1; Sandford, 1957), thus evading the fear of loneliness and separation. It has been speculated that the often tremendous pain and anxiety experienced by a dying patient result from the absence of the possibility of forming a transference with another human being and that "denial, anxiety, depression, increased narcissism and apathy, may be a result of actual or anticipated object loss and are by no means intrinsic to the psychological response to death" (Norton, 1963, p. 559).

CASE 1: THE DEATH OF AN OLD WOMAN

COURSE OF THE ILLNESS

Diagnosis: Carcinoma adenomatosum cardiae inoperata cum metastases hepatis.

A tumor of the cardiac region was perceptible in X-ray examinations of the esophagus performed because the patient was having difficulty in swallowing. A biopsy taken during esophagoscopy established adenocarcinoma of the ventricular cardiae. Gamma examination of the liver a month later revealed enlargement of the left lobe and extensive metastases in the right one. Medication was then begun, with Fluoro-Uracil administered in three successive stages. A year later swallowing had become more difficult, obstructing eating, and ventricle X-ray examination revealed a tumorous growth extending from the cardia as far as the great span of the ventricle up half way to the corpus, and in the esophagus as high as 10 cm from the cardia. Gastrotomy was performed. The patient received no specific treatment thereafter, but her general condition was stabilized by liquid and red-cell transfusion. A steady weakening followed for a period of three months, and the patient died after suffering from the illness for about a year and a half.

THE PATIENT'S LIFE HISTORY

I shall call my patient Aino. She was the youngest in her family, and had two older brothers and one older sister. Her father was a well-paid skilled laborer, and her mother was a full-time housewife. When Aino was 10 years old her mother quite unexpectedly died of heart infarction while in the sauna.

In Aino's memories her mother remained idealized for her patience and beauty. After her mother's death, Aino's father took care of the family with the help of the older children, and Aino liked to think that she had not really suffered a loss by her mother's death "because father took her place as well as his own."

Aino went to school, finishing the middle grade of high school, and after that stayed at home to take care of her father because her brothers had already gone off to work and her sister had left home to continue her studies. A couple of years later Aino also took a job, but she continued to live with her father until his death. When she was 22, he was accidentally killed, suffocated by smoke while rescuing people from a fire. The father's heroic death and her own idealization of his deed led to a memory of him as a supernatural and awe-inspiring person far above any ordinary man.

At the time of her father's death, Aino had a steady relationship with a young man of her own age, but she now put a very sudden end to it, and instead began to see a man 14 years her senior. They were married after a year's courtship. He resembled her father in some ways, was also a skilled laborer, and, what was more important, Aino was much intrigued because he came from a poor family where the children had sometimes known hunger. He had been forced to go to work at the age of 10, and had worked his way to a skilled occupation. He greatly admired his own mother who, despite poverty, had been very tender to her children and, in addition to 10 of her own, had taken on the care of two orphans. Her husband's skill in playing the violin was also significant for Aino.

The marriage was a happy one. At 25 Aino gave birth to a girl. During delivery she lost consciousness; the doctor later told her that the cause had been her "too small heart," and that she could never undergo another pregnancy. She never did have another child, and was always afraid that her heart would fail whenever she was under physical strain or when she occasionally lost her temper.

Her husband was pensioned at the age of 57 after an accident. His skull was fractured in an automobile collision, and his sight was so badly impaired that he could not continue to work. This was followed by a deep depression, with paranoid fears of either political or moral-religious persecution. Caring for her husband seemed too much of a strain to Aino, but their daughter's leaving home to study elsewhere coincided with this hardship, and Aino found that listening to her husband's recurrent fantasies of fear was, after all, a meaningful task.

Aino had worked all her life in the same office, where she had been given training as a clerk. She had a steady job, but during the economic depression in the thirties she had been laid off twice for a period of a year. She had resented this because she considered herself one of the most capable employees in the office; she was always consulted whenever help was needed. She took great pains and worked overtime a great deal in order to keep this position. Her husband had worked for the same employer, as had her father in his time, and it had been her father's wish that she take the job. She had also found her best friends among the office staff, although she was above office gossip and never engaged in the usual small talk. Her one important hobby was reciting poetry; she spent a great deal of time on it, and was always willing to perform at charity balls.

The relationship between Aino and her daughter was a warm and close one without Aino's trying in any way to bind the girl to herself. She encouraged her daughter in her studies as well as in her artistic pursuits. The daughter achieved an academic degree. However, in her senior school years she had dropped her musical activities after having performed with her mother for many years, and, as Aino put it, "this was the greatest sorrow in my life." By living frugally and denying herself many things, Aino had made it possible for her daughter to achieve social well-being.

ONSET OF THE ILLNESS

Aino was pensioned in the spring following a winter during which she had suffered from urinary bladder inflammation that had been treated with drugs. Earlier she had always been healthy except for the loss of consciousness, first in childbirth, another time after a tiring hike, and a third time when she missed the chance to look after her grandchild while her daughter was getting a divorce. Cardiological examination later on revealed no organic lesion, nor did she have any heart trouble in her older age.

Being pensioned was no easy change of life for her, a fact of which she was fully aware, for she feared the pensioner's idle and meaningless life. However, when the time came to retire at the age of 63, she quit working and refrained from asking for more time. Her motive for this decision was that it was "better to go than beg for extra time," for she felt that she could no longer work as efficiently as had been her habit.

As a pensioner Aino spent six months in her city home and at the summer cottage, not traveling anywhere else and confining herself to the company of her husband and her widowed sister. She took care of these two close relatives, giving both of them much good advice about the future; for her daughter she even drew up a written training program. At this time she suffered from urinary difficulties and from a feeling of heaviness at the bottom of her abdomen, ailments that she considered a good excuse for cutting herself off from the rest of the world. Late in the autumn her sister fell ill with pancreatitis. She was in very poor condition, a suspicion of cancer arose, and a fatal outcome was even feared. While nursing her sister during the winter months, Aino got a thrombosis in her leg. She had also noted some difficulty in swallowing of short duration, and therefore she went to see a doctor. Medical examination completed by the end of February showed that she had gastric cancer, and she was told of the fact then and there.

PSYCHOTHERAPY

Aino came to me for treatment as soon as she learned of her illness because, having read some of my articles on the subject, she knew that I treated cancer patients with psychotherapy. Aino lived quite far away, and therefore she came to my office once or twice a week at the beginning of therapy, but after her admission to the hospital in Helsinki I went to see her four to five times a week. With the exception of a six weeks' break during the summer months, therapy continued regularly and lasted altogether a year and three months. With Aino's consent I also talked with her husband and daughter about her.

Phase I: Waiting for Admission to the Hospital

Aino had been prescribed mild sedatives while she was waiting for the examination results, but she stopped taking them when the result — cancer — was disclosed to her. Her first reaction was one of grief and of weeping by herself. This lasted a few days. Aino's own account of the preceding events was that the doctor who had made all the tests and had undertaken the examination in the first place had sent her to another doctor for surgery, and that he, in turn, had sent her back again, claiming that he could not perform surgery without a full report of laboratory tests. She described how the first doctor had been annoyed and had told her that he could certainly do the tests all over again but that it was no use because she didn't have a chance to live anyway. Aino now turned her back on both doctors in the district and came to Helsinki to the Radiotherapy Clinic. Here the fact was confirmed that surgery would be of no use, and she was given radiotherapy instead.

During the period of some weeks while she waited for admission to the hospital, Aino was quite active and felt no undue anxiety. She was preparing for death, her experience being that, after the first reaction of grief, the knowledge of the nature of her illness—cancer—had eased the depression that had lasted the many months of her life as a pensioner and as a nurse to her ill sister. She did not notice the difficulty in swallowing any more. Summoning all her strength in her worry over her husband's future, she made plans for him to go to a nursing home; she made detailed arrangements for the management of the household, and drew up plans for house-keeping. After that, she began to clean cupboards and to tidy up her home, saying, "I'm not going to leave the cleaning for anyone else to do."

She looked after herself very carefully, dutifully obeying doctor's orders, and wishing to eat only the most wholesome food. The problem of eating solid food because swallowing had again become difficult she denied by rationalizing that food in liquid form was lighter and more nourishing and gave her more energy. She felt that losing weight made her look younger, an opinion shared by her acquaintances and rela-tives. In other words, she denied the "badness" of her illness by emphasizing the good things still left in her life. This approach was even reflected in attempts to make her home look "younger"; she bought new rugs and curtains of pale blue and pink to replace the old, darker ones. She wanted to leave a pretty home behind.

Aino was bewildered by the changes she seemed to notice in her daughter and her sister. She thought that her sister's grave illness had brought about the change, making her friendlier and less inclined to harp on trivial matters. She found her daughter much happier than before. Aino felt that she had found new values in life now that she loved her family more intensely than before, and that she could lavish her love on others.

Aino seemed to have much more time for herself now, and she was ready to spend more time and more money. She bought her family presents, even presents for her grandchildren's future communion. She began to reread novels that had been part of her youthful interests and the poetry that had been her favorite. All in all, she felt that she now had the right to enjoy herself.

At this stage of psychotherapy I listened and asked some neutral questions, but for the most part Aino was intent on talking spontaneously about herself. She had the feeling that she was making me a present of her life's experience, and she was indeed a charming donator. She would repeat the sentence: "If only I can live over the summer and enjoy summertime once more." My comment to this—"surely"—she took as a magic promise; "The doctor always knows best."

Phase II: Hospitalization during the Wait for Summer

On admission to the hospital Aino had undergone a transformation. She looked younger, both in her choice of clothes and in her hairdo. She talked about the literature of her youth, which reflected the virginal morals of her girlhood, and compared it with the sexual morals of present-day youth. She disapproved of young people "living together not being even properly engaged." She herself had been "a one-man woman," and she was happy about it now. She talked about her parents and the great love there had been between them. She kept in her handbag a photograph of her parents taken at the time of their engagement; she looked at it often and admired her father's good looks. She thought she resembled her mother very much; "Father said as much when he was living." Her appearance at this time was that of a bride preparing for her wedding. She told me how astonished she had been at hearing another patient say on leaving the hospital to go home that she was going to give her husband a good scolding if her favorite plant had died because he had forgotten to water it. Aino said, "In my present state things like that have no meaning at all; I have put earthly matters behind."

Tests and examinations as well as nursing care appeared to distress her; she did not believe they could be of any help in curing her, although she did believe pain could be avoided by these means. She wanted me to support this belief, and I gave her my reassurance. She refused to take any "leukemia drugs," which had caused another patient to lose her hair, because it was very important now to look as nice as possible.

Aino pondered over the cause of cancer and said that no one in her family had ever had the illness and all had lived to an old age. (This was not true; both her parents and one brother had died in middle age, but she overlooked that fact.) She supposed that the cancer was caused by some external factor, her reason being that "there are so many artificial substances added to food even, and it may also be polluted," and that "the cancer appeared so suddenly, without any warning." In other words, she felt the illness had an external origin.

After spending little more than a week in the hospital, Aino was overtaken by depression after attending a lecture for medical students at which she was the patient under demonstration. She felt she was being accused of something when the students asked her questions like "Why had she not sought medical care earlier?"; "Did she not have any premonitions because of her earlier pains and ailments?"; "How often had she had medical examinations?" She felt depressed because she could not find satisfactory answers to all these questions, she blamed herself for having neglected the early signs of the illness, and she was afraid the doctors would be angered by her negligence. She found no fault with doctors; on the contrary, she exaggerated the care her own private doctor had taken of her. But she did find fault with stingy, rich people, and she hoped that some day they would come to realize that money cannot buy anything of true value, that "money could not open the gates of heaven." At this time she "celebrated" her fortieth wedding anniversary by donating a considerable sum of money to a children's home. For my part, I performed the role of a listener, and my comment on her depression was that she wished to be good to everyone, even the medical students, because she wanted her ideal of goodness to be fulfilled in the best possible way, that her own demands that she please everyone caused her self-reproaches, and the natural curiosity of the students seemed like a reproach to her. When she understood this explanation quite clearly, her depression lifted.

With the depression over, Aino gathered her strength and plunged into creativity activity. She began to prepare tape recordings of the poems she had recited, to be given to her daughter as a Mother's Day present. She took great pains to choose and to experiment with various combinations of poems, rehearsing them with me, and I did my best to support her in her activity. The completion of the tape was of great emotional value to her, and she told her daughter that "now she would never forget her mother's recitals nor her voice, for they were in good keeping." Her mood was elevated partly by this experience and partly by a new type of medicine that had been administered to her at the same time. She had a strong belief in the strengthening effect of the drug. She felt she had been able to "extend her life span."

Now that Aino had been capable of a creative act that would preserve a part of her for the world in the form of the tape, she began to recall memories she had previously resisted. She had never talked about her mother's death with anyone; instead, at the time, when she was 10 years old, the mother's goodness had been praised, and it had been emphatically stated that heaven was a good place for her. Aino's actual mourning had never been worked through. She could remember how her mother had slumped down while tying her shoelaces, and afterwards had lain motionless with the children around her. She had believed that her mother was asleep. People were crying and her mother was carried away. She had seen her father crying and saying to himself and his children that "now Mother is happy in heaven," and that "now I can be both mother and father to Aino." She could remember how she, too, had wanted to cry, but had been afraid of offending her father, and had also wanted to think that her father could take her mother's place. Aino had denied her grief in childhood, and she could not remember ever having missed her mother later on. Not until now did she miss her mother, and now she would have liked to talk with her about her own illness and threatening death. She found consolation in the thought that now her daughter could take her mother's place. She talked confidentially about these matters with her daughter.

By this time Aino had lost a great deal of weight, and palpation of her abdomen indicated that the tumor had grown. She had been in the habit of closely observing the growth of the tumor from the very beginning, and she wanted me to check it, fearing that it might block the larynx. She could still swallow and eat fairly well. But her liver had now begun to expand. This worried her much more because, not understanding the function of the liver, the unknown frightened her, and she was afraid that the enlargement of the liver would lead to poisoning. She believed that the tumor could be extracted by surgery.

At her own request Aino was allowed to go to her summer cottage to spend the longed-for summer there. I did not see her again for about six weeks.

Phase III: Hoping for a Miraculous Recovery

Aino spent the summer weeks with her husband and her sister at the summer cottage. She was relaxed and allowed the others to wait on her. She read novels and seemed to enjoy herself, and she was filled with kindness and generosity toward her family. She told them to take anything they wanted in the cottage, and made plans for the sale of the cottage when this last summer was over because her husband must not come there alone lest he drown in the lake. He had once fallen in the lake, but had been able to rescue himself without anyone's help. He had now developed a deep depression with the same paranoid fears that had been manifest when he had been pensioned. But this time Aino put up a resistance to his monotonous complaints.

When Aino came back to the hospital after the summer, it was found that her liver had diminished in size, and she thought that a "miracle" had occurred, hopefully thinking of recovering in a miraculous way. She thought her recovery was the outcome of the happy and gay state of mind that had over-taken her during the summer; in other words, that the cancer had been cured by her own good emotions.

A month later, after a short stay at home, she sank back into her hospital bed in fatigue, saying she had no more strength left to think about her family: "My husband has the nursing home, and the others don't need me." Her interest in the external world diminished; she wanted to talk mostly about her sick body, about the development of the illness and the ways the cancer could be treated. Her interest focused more and more on herself. For long periods she would keep silent, looking me sharply in the eyes in a clinging, imploring way. There was a gentle demand in her look that seemed fearful, as if she were weighing my trustworthiness.

A new doctor assigned to Aino's ward wanted to put things in order, and, according to Aino, he had told her that her liver was so frail that it might burst, and at the same time had asked her if she would not rather go to the hospital in her own home town. Aino protested vehemently, and hate surged in her toward the new doctor, whom she found at fault and blamed constantly. While her hatred was aimed at him, her attachment to me grew. She was happy when I brought her flowers, and a mimosa a friend gave her reawakened a poem in her mind, one she had often recited in her youth and which she now called the "Mimosa Poem." She could remember parts of the poem that made her realize how well it reflected her own mood. The poem was "In the Graveyard" ("Hautausmaalla"), by Oiva Paloheimo:

> The teacher, a childlike old man,
> In old age still loved his natural history,
> The beetles, and above all, of course, the moss,
> And . . . and all
> That's part of natural history.

> —"About time the teacher,"
> The deaconess would worry,
> "Give more time to the most important.
> In good time remember: From the earth thou . . ."
> —"From the earth," mused the old man, "ay, important
>   it is."

> And so now on his knees
> He leaned on a grave with fingers crossed.
> For in the palm of his hand
> He hid a mimosa, a live young flower.
> And in the middle of the graveyard!

> Then Death took a step
> To the grave beside the teacher
> And heedlessly inquired:
> "Are your accounts closed,
> Have you said your prayers?"

> The teacher, somewhat ashamed
> —"No . . . not a prayer this,
> This is a mimosa, you see . . ."
> Death, ashamed he too,

But then with curiosity
Bent his head at the teacher's side.
And the teacher described to him
How the petals when evening comes
—like this—gather together,
And at nightfall the flower bends
And looks straight down—this way—
Like the lamp in the study at home.

Late into the night still wandering and crouching
In the graveyard, two stooping old men,
Ever more radiantly
They enthused and discussed—
The life of flowers.

Aino wanted to learn the poem again by heart, and I helped her. She repeated it many times, and thought the poet had found a good subject for the poem. She reflected that in the face of death one need not be humble if one possessed rich and dear memories like hers, for she had loved and cared for her family. I supported her in these thoughts, saying that even death could be discussed as in the Mimosa Poem, and then one was not alone any more. Aino felt this was true.

When her daughter visited her the same day, Aino gave her wedding ring to her, explaining how unique it was and how she could have it remade for herself. At the same time they talked about the times when they had performed together during the girl's school years, the mother reciting poetry and the daughter playing the piano. Aino then told her daughter how great a disappointment it had been when she had suddenly refused to participate, and how this event had been the subject of a newspaper article. Not until now was Aino ready to forgive her daughter.

This happened three months before Aino's death. She had a feeling that she would not live long, but she still hoped to spend Christmas at home.

It has already been mentioned that Aino had stopped worrying about her husband, and he did not come to visit her in the hospital during her last weeks. Instead he wrote letters or made phone calls. When she had received a letter from him telling her that he was bringing her bad news on his next visit, Aino thought that someone had died or that he was seriously ill. When he did arrive, he was very regressed and dizzy, supporting himself on the walls when he walked toward her. The bad news consisted of his having fallen down on the street, having been taken to a hospital in a state of coma, and having spent the night there. When Aino heard this she was very angry and forbade him to visit her in the hospital, her reason being that she could not stand the worry and the fear that something might happen to him on the way. At the same time she perceived that her husband's regressive entreaty awakened an unendurable hatred in her that she wanted to avoid.

While her husband was the target of her anger, I became the object of her growing feelings of attachment, feelings that were those of a little girl happy about our relationship, with no trace of adult eroticism. She had succeeded in keeping my flowers fresh for 10 days, and, making an error in time, told me that the flowers had not wilted in her care for a whole month, "which is a wonder." Her thoughts returned to the "Mimosa Poem," and she made comparisons between our companionship and the prolongation of her life. She also wondered what she would give me as a birthday present, and revealed her wish that her life could be prolonged by thinking about presents because they revived the good emotions. In other words, Aino believed that cherishing a present and giving one would add to her days.

Just before leaving for Christmas vacation, Aino was rather regressed and mournful, and her speech became a mutter. She talked about her will because she was afraid that her husband would donate everything to the church, as he had threatened to do in a passing depressed mood and in his great fear of persecution by priests. She asked me to bring her a favorite delicacy, salted fish, and ate it in silence and in deep thought just before going home.

Phase IV: The Last Two Months

When Aino returned from her short Christmas visit home, she told me that she had left home for good, and did not wish to leave the hospital again. Thereafter she did not leave her bed often; swallowing had become very difficult for her, and the occasional pains in her stomach had grown more intense. At times she would lie in her bed with an expressionless face and look at me with very searching eyes. She was aware that death was near, but she felt no anxiety, no fear or open hatred anymore; instead, a growing apathy had overcome her. In an unemotional way she talked about the world as a bad place: about the obstacles in the way of children in their competition in a relentless society, about the violence the young manifested in attacking old people, about parents' neglect of their children.

Her mind was focused on her own body and the pain. She was afraid the pain might become worse, but she still hoped to be helped by surgery. When the decision was finally made to perform a gastrotomy and she was told the date, she became very frightened and anxious. She wanted to be treated mainly for somatic ailments, and hoped to die during the operation because, as she said, "When the end is near anyway, I could be free from all further suffering." The aftereffects of the operation were very difficult, and it did not bring the anticipated alleviation of her pains. She could swallow only drops of water. During an X-ray examination she had panicked in the dark room and screamed that she was dying of thirst.

Open fear of death now burst through her defenses, and overt primitive rage was directed at the hospital staff. She blamed them all for neglect of their duties, for poor care of patients in general, and for prevailing unconcern. By this time she was being given only fluids by transfusion, and the inability to eat and drink represented a deep narcissistic offense to her. She said, "I am like some object that is filled and that has no will of its own." Her affectionate emotions were directed to her family and to me, and she spoke lovingly of her husband, calling him "dear papa." She fantasied that he would not live long after her death. She was fond of recalling pleasant memories from the past with her family, but her sincerest wish was to die "before all the difficulties started again." Among these she included not only the pain itself, but emotions of hate and the anticipation of the unknown.

She told me of a dream she had had. "I was in Denmark, there were many strange people, they spoke a language I did not understand. They sold porno pictures there, and offered me some, too. It felt bad and I was afraid." The dream had bewildered her, because she had never been in Denmark, nor had she ever looked at pornographic pictures. My interpretation of this was that she apparently pondered over everything that was strange and incomprehensible in death, feeling it to be something akin to the alien sensation caused by pornography in her youth. The interpretation seemed very plausible to her and gave her reason to trust me. She put it in so many words: "It feels really good when someone else knows something one doesn't understand."

Apathy had vanished, and Aino began to verbalize her fear of death to me and to her family; it made her feel good to be able to approach another human being, even though death was now her only concern. She thought she was going to die too young, and considered it an injustice, asking, "Why should it be me?" She blamed me for having lied to her when I had said that pain need not necessarily be part of the disease. She felt strangely tired and could not understand the reason for it. It was something strange and frightening.

Aino found it odd, too, that although she was not eating or

drinking orally, she was still alive owing to the transfusion of necessary fluids. Occasionally she hallucinated, and one night she had a hallucination that she must get some pepper and bread crumbs, and, being very stubborn about it, she got the goodhearted nurse on night duty to bring her the crumbs. Afterwards she was very frightened by the episode, feeling that both the nurse and she herself were mad. She perceived her own fear of insanity, and it was a cause of great concern because she was afraid she might say something to her daughter that she did not really mean. She was also very concerned about her daughter, fearing that she might be attacked on the street or have an accident of some kind.

In this phase of Aino's death process, some weeks before the end, she was overcome by strong grief. She wept and mourned because in a short time she would not see her family, particularly her daughter and grandchildren, her grandchildren would not see her any more, she was withering away, her body no longer obeyed her, and so on. She was angry with me because I could not help her to keep the painful grief away; all I could do was to agree with her that grief was painful. She had a nightmare in which she had in great anxiety asked a nurse to bring her a bag for the salt she had. My interpretation of the nightmare was that she still wished to find a place to put herself, and she then felt that she had been understood. Then she asked that her life should not be prolonged by any mechanical means.

During the last two weeks she hallucinated, was occasionally aggressive and occasionally dependent. She wanted her daughter to feed her some salted fish, but she was no longer able to eat it; her inability to make the slightest effort left her in a state of helpless submission, and she demanded that a member of her family sit by her bedside. When she was seized by fear she would tell the person who was with her about it. She dreamed that she was being forcibly taken away from the hospital. When on waking she described the dream, she was very relieved to find that it was not yet true. Another nightmare, indefinable and horrifying, that repeatedly haunted her was of "something being cut and then put together again." When there was no one with her she would call me on the phone and talk in a hallucinating way, but when I answered her she was able to collect herself and her logical thinking and rational speech, as she did when I visited her in the hospital. Her hallucinations focused on her childhood memories, her childhood home and mother, on swimming, and on the imaginary vision of the two of us going somewhere on a train.

When she was angry she would scold people because she wasn't good enough for them, and then she would try to speak in a very refined manner. She blamed people for their selfishness in "just sitting there and letting her do all the talking in her weak condition." The general idea of her angry thoughts was that too much was expected of her, and she would burst out crying in agony for help. After her bed had been fitted with higher sides because of her restlessness and the danger of her falling off, she warned everyone not to come too close because "she was supposed to be a dangerous alcoholic."

During Aino's last days her affection and her hatred were directed at her family and at me. She never mentioned having any visions of life after death. All her emotions were directed at the people caring for her, and occasionally they became the objects of her regressively experienced past. She moaned in pain and agony to her sister sitting at her bedside until she lost consciousness a little more than an hour before she died.

SUMMARY OF THE CASE

In the foregoing I have described the emotional interaction in the case without linking it to any theory or trying to draw any conclusions. In the following I shall set forth the conclusions I reached in the therapy.

The Object Relations of the Patient

At the time of her death the patient was a married woman of 65. In her preadolescence she had lost her own mother through death, and had not been able to accomplish mourning work after this bereavement. Instead, by ego defense against the pain of mourning, by repression of the ambivalence of the emotional conflict, she had created an idealized image of the lost mother, and had adopted a trusting belief that her father could replace her mother completely. When her father met his death in heroic circumstances, her idealization of the lost parent was still further enhanced. After her father's death she left the young man who had been her steady companion, and chose another love object, a man many years her senior, whom she married. Her relationship to her husband was one of idealization on the one hand and of protection and caring on the other. She had partly replaced the lost father by her husband, and had partly identified with the lost father. To be more exact, she had identified with the fused father-mother image that had been formed in preadolescence when the father had taken the mother's place in caring for the young girl.

The patient's opinion of her father's reaction to the loss of his wife was that he had denied the full meaning of the loss and had adopted the mother's role in the family. It had been a successful resolution as far as the preoedipally based needs of the patient were concerned — needs for security, care, concern, tenderness, etc. Oedipal identification with the mother who is the object of the father's erotic love, and rivalry with the mother to win the object of love had been thwarted in prepuberty when the mother died. This was reflected in the patient's neurotic fears that became manifest at childbirth, when a baby girl was born, and in the oedipal rivalry. The patient was afraid of death, and later with exaggerated resignation she did her utmost to support her daughter in succeeding as a woman. She achieved recognition in her work and enjoyed her own ability to take care of others, but the rivalry and the necessity of pushing oneself forward were so frightening that she relinquished her job. The same pattern appeared in her artistic activities. She developed herself and gave performances as long as her daughter in her girlhood and preadolescence participated in these activities, but when the girl lost interest she gave up the hobby, although she was very much disappointed and experienced a great loss.

The loss of her job, temporarily during the economic depression and finally when she was pensioned, was a trying experience for the patient. In her work she had conformed to the ideology of serving others, an ideology that was partly based on an identification with the idealized father-mother image and had partly taken the place of her parents. She did not leave her job gradually and mournfully; instead, she summoned her courage and wrenched herself free of her dependence on her job that in many ways unconsciously paralleled the lost and unmourned object relations of her childhood. In her state of depression after the losses she sought a sufferer by proxy by helping others who were in poor condition and in need of care, simultaneously denying her own weakened state.

Mobilization of Good Emotions

When she had been informed of the nature of her illness and impending death (Phase I), after the first shock had passed the patient reacted by taking refuge with her family and her therapist. The depression that had been brought on by the feeling of isolation after being pensioned was then eased. She had the experience of being loved and of finding new values in life. She felt she was more at liberty to express her libidinal emotions, which she now mobilized. Rivalry and envy lost their meaning for her and her closest relatives seemed to have changed, the change having been brought about by her own good emotions. Through idealization of other people and their instructions, which she carefully obeyed, she experienced having attained secondary narcissistic value. She was loved because she loved others, she was given to because she gave to others. At this stage, the patient strove to handle the narcissistic offense of the illness by idealization, i.e., by the libidinal version of the *lex talionis* of the oedipal phase, good for good. Mobilized narcissistic libido was then gradually directed straight to the sublimated form of woman's inner space — to her own home, to the decoration of her home and herself, as well as to her own body as a whole.

When libido became increasingly attached to herself, it made possible the maintenance and even the increase of her narcissistic value, in contrast to the progressing illness and the gradual destruction of her body (Phases I-IV). Simultaneously libido was withdrawn from external object relations, at first from objects of lesser importance, and later from everyone except family members and therapist. When the patient relinquished her objects, she at first mobilized her libido toward the object and felt that it was more valuable than before, and then she acquired an auxiliary ego by giving her instructions to another person (Phases I-II). In her experience the auxiliary ego became a continuation of her own significance to the object, and she was able to withdraw her libido from the object to fortify her own narcissism.

Phallic Defense against Fear of Death

In this phase of therapy (Phase II) the patient used the therapist not only as a transference object for the mobilized libidinal fantasies, but also as a magic protection against the fear of death. On one unconscious level she experienced the therapist as a phallic father image who provided her with phallic power and knowledge for continuing her life in exchange for herself and her life's experience. On the conscious level she expressed disapproval of the erotic relationships of modern youth that contrasted with the idealized innocence of her own youth and the "pure" love of her own parents. Unconsciously, the protection phallic love could offer had multiple value for the patient. First, the romantic love for the therapist, who was experienced as phallicly magical, gave the protection of a good emotion against death. Second, the idea that she could enter into the erotic relationship of her parents would erase the envy and hatred at having been left alone and outside the oedipal situation. The patient carried her parents' engagement picture in her handbag. Third, the parents were dead, the separation mourning had contained the element of their idealized mutual love, and thus the patient could resort to the same pattern of idealization as a magical ritual, as a sort of phallic protection against the pain of separation. Fourth, in the patient's mind "pure" love would guarantee the psychic constancy of love while the body was ravaged by the illness; in other words, eroticization of emotions and memories would compensate for the lacking means of physical erotic attraction.

Fifth, oedipal rivalry in itself contained fear of death and fear of punishment, and therefore the patient tried to mobilize phallicly a magic protection against fear of death and fantasies of rivalry. She experienced cancer as an external evil, even as a pollution, and she laid great emphasis on the purity of her parents as far as cancer was concerned. Her attitude toward cancer was in many respects reminiscent of her attitude toward oedipal rivalry. She denied the idea that either originated within herself. Possibly she experienced cancer as a punishment for the unconscious oedipal hate that her strong superego endeavored to keep in rein. This finds confirmation in the way in which the defense built on phallic fantasies crumbled. The phallic fantasies were not part of her own ability; rather, they were used as a defense against the external world. The fantasied defense broke down when she could not meet the demands of her superego in the instance of the medical students asking her questions. She was overcome by fear that she was no longer favored by those protecting her phallicly. Self-accusations of the oedipal phase got the upper hand and depression then followed.

Creativity as a Means of Abolishing Separation Anxiety

When the realization that external, phallic, magical support had forsaken her, after a depressive episode the patient mobilized her creative capacities. A characteristic quality of her creative activity was in finding fulfillment in a relationship of two; in other words, she must find fulfillment with another or for another. The object of active creativity (Phase II) would continue to exist and to remind another person of her even after her death. Creative interaction in the therapeutic relationship-between-two revived memories of the preadolescent period, until then repressed, that were connected with the loss of the mother. With the support of the therapist she could now work through some of the mourning, could understand her mother, and could identify with her. Remembering her mother and her therapist and enjoying the company of her family during the summer months were enriching experiences that fortified her ego during the break in the therapy.

After the vacation, she had the experience of being miraculously cured (Phase III), but the progressing illness proved the opposite. Her strength waning, and reality indicating that cure was impossible, the hate that surged in her mind was aimed at the doctor responsible for her care, and she became more attached to her therapist. In her mind the therapeutic interaction became the intimate relationship between two people, the interaction between patient and therapist representing a strongly cathected repetition of past relationships-between-two. She remembered a long-forgotten poem, "In the Graveyard," from the past, in which death is transformed into a friend by the subject's creative impulse, the mimosa. In a regressive way she combined her thoughts about the poem, about her past, and about the therapy relationship into a unity, and she felt that the creativity of the relationship, mutual giving and taking, was a sustaining force in life. At the same time she was able to work through her disappointment over the break in the mutual creative activity of mother and daughter. Furthermore, she could transfer her hope for a "miracle," earlier connected with hope of recovery, to the maintenance of the creative therapy relationship-between-two. The flowers brought by the therapist and the fact that they stayed fresh for a long time in her care were significant symbols of the relationship and the miracle.

Additionally, discussions about death with the therapist brought the fantasy of personified death closer (Phase III). The patient had the experience of conversing with death while talking to her therapist, the experience paralleling that of the poem "In the Graveyard." The transference relationship created the illusion of death as being personified in the therapist, and she felt that by tending to this relationship, by giving presents to the therapist, this creative illusion of communication with death would surely prolong her life.

Regression to Complete Dependency

During the last two months the pains increased and the patient gradually regressed further, her libido becoming more and more attached to thoughts about her own body. In this phase she sought the care of other people (Phase IV). At first, aggressions were aimed at objects that were not connected with important object relations of the moment. When surgery proved to be ineffective and her inability to eat any longer had led to disappointment, open fear of death overcame her. She still hoped to find a way to die of her own will and to avoid the ultimate submission to her own helplessness. The archaic hate of early infancy for one's total helplessness was aimed at the people caring for her, at the very people who showed their affection for her and from whom she sought care. The splitting of emotions toward various objects could be observed only momentarily.

Death as an unknown existence roused the patient's fear (Phase IV). She tried at first to understand the fear of the unknown on the basis of past and already clarified fears. She hoped to find a model for solution in the childhood fear of the mysterious sexual organs that had been reflected in the fear of pornography and that had already been solved. In this fear of the unknown, she was able to turn for help to her therapist and other people caring for her. At rare lonely moments hallucinations overcame the patient, and she felt that she could trust no one, as in the instance when the nurse on duty complied with her hallucinatory wishes and brought her the bread crumbs she had asked for. She was capable of returning to a level of reality if supported by another person. Thus the hallucinations took the place of human relations in the patient's mind and could be expelled by the ego support of the therapist or someone else. The patient's fear of insanity was closely connected with the fear of being left alone and the fear that, alone without outside ego support, her ego would disintegrate, and she would go mad and not understand anything any more. Another source of the fear of insanity was the fear that her own hate would destroy the person caring for her, foremostly her own daughter. Behind this fear was also the unconscious wish to die together with someone close, with a member of the family. No attempt was made to explain death to the patient. She was convinced that death was a state of unknown existence. She avoided the excessive feeling of loneliness by turning to interactive relations with her family and therapist. Talking about death, expressing emotions of grief, affection, and aggression toward people she trusted, could all minimize the separation anxiety.

The patient's libidinal hallucinations that were attached to human relations, mostly to the relationship with her mother, included childhood memories she had internalized. During the dying process she had mournfully approached her losses—loss of home, loss of family, loss of her own body, loss of her creativity—and she had regressed to the experience of being totally dependent on the care of others. Relinquishing had not been accomplished by identification with and internalization of features of the lost object, but rather by substitution of the people caring for and understanding her as the regression advanced. She had regressed to dependency on people to whom she had externalized earlier internalized qualities of the caring mother. Finally, she had internalized the care of her therapist and her family, and experienced death as a regressive togetherness with them.

CASE 2: A MAN'S DEATH IN MID-LIFE[1]

Somatic Illness

Carcinoma of the right testis (Carcinoma embryonale anaplastica testis dextris cum metastatibus lymphoglandulae parailiaca et para-aortae) had been diagnosed one year and seven months before the patient died. At the time the disease was discovered, metastases had developed in the lymphatic nodes of the femoral vein and aorta region. At the time of the patient's death, there were numerous metastases in all parts of the body, e.g., the left lung was completely infiltrated by carcinomatous growth.

---

[1] Co-authored with Maija-Liisa Vauhkonen. Vauhkonen was the psychotherapist, and Hägglund the supervisor of the therapy.

The Patient's Life History

The patient, whom I shall call Juha, was a man of 29, the middle child of a large family. His father was a state official in a high position, and his mother a housewife with a high-school education. The patient had not finished high school, but had managed to attend college for two years, without, however, completing his studies. Service in the army had been completed faultlessly. After acquiring a job, he kept on working for the same employer and made good progress. He had married a girl somewhat his senior, who had studied the same subjects as he had and worked in the same field as he did. The couple had no children.

The patient had pleasant memories of his childhood, although there had been conflicts between his parents regarding child rearing, and the atmosphere in the home had been unharmonious. His father was very stern, expecting the boy to succeed at school and to attain an academic degree and high social status as well. The father was not given to showing his feelings impulsively, but would indicate his benevolence by some reward and his offended feelings by severe punishment, such as excluding the boy from the family circle, not allowing him, for instance, to partake of meals. The patient described his relationship with his father as involving hate on his part, and said that the values his father held high were worthless in his own eyes. The mother, who was tender and understanding with her children, tried to ease the conflict-ridden relations between her family members, and very often made herself the target of the father's anger and abuse. The patient remembered always having been his mother's favorite, and the relationship remained a close one even in adulthood. His relationship to his sisters was a good and close one, but he never got along very well with his brother. He disapproved of his brother in a moral sense, and wanted to have nothing to do with him. Thus it came about that he generally approved of the women in the family while morally condemning and avoiding the men.

The relationship between the patient and his wife was basically warm and close. There had been some conflicts in the marriage at the beginning, and an estrangement had begun to creep in, but the patient's illness had brought about a change, and the two were then able to find a new way of approaching each other. There was a tendency to withdraw in the patient's character. He was well liked by his colleagues, and the conflicts about authority in his private life were not reflected at his place of work. In his work the patient tended to be very independent, whereas in his private life he submitted to decisions and resolutions made by others. He himself felt that his self-esteem was somewhat low because of his severely moral self-discipline.

As a child the patient had been shy and timid, and had suffered from acrophobia that had continued even into adulthood. As an adult he suffered from periods of insomnia and depression. He was jealous of his wife and blamed himself for it, seeing it as a sign of his own restrictedness. At the time of the onset of the illness he felt that his mental state was poor, suffered from neurotic conflicts, and had, in fact, often felt the need to see a psychiatrist because of the tension he felt and the chronic, allergic colds he had. However, he had never actually taken the decisive step.

ONSET OF THE ILLNESS

Before the onset of the illness, the patient had been physically healthy. Upon discovering the lump in one of his testes, the patient was frightened and thought that he had contracted a venereal disease, although he could not understand how it could have happened. The fleeting thought that it might be a malignant growth also passed through his mind. He postponed consulting a doctor in an effort to forget the whole thing. But when he heard of a friend his own age dying after cancer surgery, his fright became unbearable. At last, when four months had passed after the discovery of the lump, he consulted a doctor.

Even after the illness had been confirmed, he was afraid of surgery, fearing that he would die like his friend. His fear was even further intensified by the uncertainty he felt about his own condition. He was afraid to question the doctors attending him, and got all the information about his illness from his wife. Not until after surgery was the patient told that the tumor had been malignant. He blamed the physician who imparted the information for negligence and for having told it in a cruel way. He himself felt that he had a realistic attitude toward his illness. He considered that he was well prepared to receive the news about the nature of the illness, and in a way found the final announcement a relief. Examination had shown that metastases had spread largely to the lymphatic nodes, and therefore surgery could not be carried out as extensively as had been planned; radiotherapy was therefore considered the only possible alternative. The patient too saw that his only hope of recovery lay in radiotherapy.

Psychotherapy

The patient sought psychotherapeutic treatment well over a year after the illness had been diagnosed. At the time, he said he had had a very hard time and had been depressed and anxious. His attitude during conversation was quite positive, and he gave a frank account of himself and his life history. Investigation brought clearly to light a strong fear of death, although the patient actively denied it. He very emphatically stated to the female therapist that the male doctor who had been in charge of his care during his illness had not kept him informed of the progress of his disease, and that in fact he was not aware of it at all. The patient had chosen the therapist after an interview that had been carried out during an investigation of cancer patients because he had found the experience a positive one. It had been a strenuous effort for him to make the appointment, and he was satisfied at having overcome the obstacles. Ambivalence, already quite apparent at the beginning of therapy, persisted throughout the therapeutic relationship, and made it impossible to adhere to the original therapy contract. Instead, it was necessary to comply with the patient's wish to arrange separately for the next session each time. It was quite obvious that the patient wanted to control the therapist, and to secure the eventual possibility of leaving her to her anxiety. Therapy was, however, continued for a period of six months until the patient's death. In the beginning the patient came to the therapist's office, and later on the therapist saw him in the hospital. Usually the sessions were held every week.

Phase I: Externalization of the Superego

At the beginning of therapy, Juha mainly expressed his feelings of uncertainty about the illness, and blamed the doctors for his own ignorance of his condition and of the cause of his ailments. He complained of fatigue, insomnia, and backache, "the reason for which had not been disclosed to him." A further source of anxiety for Juha was the fact that each time he came to the outpatient clinic he was seen by a different doctor, which made him suspect that no one really knew about his case and therefore could not attend to him properly. When the therapist remarked that she understood his worry, he experienced relief. This strengthened the therapeutic alliance, and Juha was then able to externalize his strict superego to physicians. The self-accusations due to his ignorance and tardiness in seeking care were also reduced. Juha now began to express his fears, although he did not as yet verbalize them as actual fear of death. The therapist prescribed mild tranquilizers for him to take in the evening in order to fall asleep more easily, and Juha found that he was thus protected against his fear. This was the only prescription the therapist gave him, and he used the drug regularly until his death, having the prescription renewed by the physician attending to his somatic condition.

There now came an interruption in therapy, Juha having to wait two weeks because the therapist was occupied with affairs of her own. He was distinctly more anxious than usual, clearly had many physical pains, and it was with difficulty that he concentrated on the conversation when therapy was resumed. He was preoccupied by the uncertainty about the continuance of the therapy, and was relieved by the therapist's saying that the arrangement for the next therapy session would be regularly made each time in advance. A phase now followed in the therapy in which Juha described his work and his relationship to his employer in detail, apparently wanting the therapist to become thoroughly acquainted with everything that was connected with his work. Work played a central and important part in his life, and giving it up was obviously very difficult for him. He also talked about his other human relationships, especially with his father, where a change for the better had taken place after the hatred contained in it had subsided. He felt that he had begun to understand his father and his behavior better, and that lately he had even felt some sympathy for him. He talked about his school years and the time he had studied, commenting that it was so easy to talk to the therapist about his life. The objects of his hatred and his accusations continued to be the hospital staff and the hospital clergyman who, upon visiting him, had once made the usual derogatory comment about the patient's profession.

Phase II: Formation of Auxiliary Ego

On the appointed date Juha's wife called and canceled the therapy session, saying that the patient was too tired to come. Another date was set, and when Juha came he was in anguish with physical pain. Somewhat shamefacedly he disclosed that he had begun to "misuse" the tranquilizer prescribed to him. He said that he took the pill in the evening before going to bed according to instructions, but when he felt sleep over-taking him he would put up a fight against it: "It gives me a good feeling." When his wife then dozed off, he would get up and go to the couch to lie down. He described how he would lie there, listen to music, even sing to himself, sometimes just resting and daydreaming. He said that these spells in the night were a source of great satisfaction to him because pain was absent and there was nothing from the external world to disturb him. He would muse about the content of the therapy sessions, and read a great deal of literature. The book *Jonathan Livingston Seagull*, by Richard Bach, had im-pressed him deeply (the book describes the efforts of a seagull at ever more successful flights, its death, its existence after death, and its assistant in the hereafter). He mused that he could also create something like this book, that he had often thought of writing one, but had not known how to go about it. He grieved that there was no more time left, and that he would lose the chance of creating something personal and permanent because "I had to fall ill and give up everything so early in life." He now verbalized his sorrow at approaching death during the therapy session. — The atmosphere during this therapy session was intensely warm and close; it was the atmosphere of the two-person relationship.

Juha's somatic condition was objectively quickly deterior-ating. His backaches returned more severely than before and bothered him very much. He again reverted to his memories of his father's stern and exacting ways as opposed to his mother's gentleness and his own exceptional position as his mother's favorite child. He plunged wholeheartedly into memories of various occasions when his mother had tried to smooth over his father's strictness and severity and to comfort Juha when he had been abused by his father.

Then Juha called and said he had been talking over his condition with his wife and that he had decided to try a sanatorium, where he was in fact now going, and he therefore wished to cancel the therapy session. But then, just before the canceled hour, his wife called and said that her husband was at home, though in such poor condition that he could not come to the therapist's office, and that he wished that she come to see him instead. This happened about three months before Juha's death. When the therapist arrived, Juha was at home alone. He seemed a bit embarrassed, and said that nothing had come of the sanatorium. His father had made the reservation and had also arranged for the transportation. On arriving at his destination Juha had become very anxious on seeing so many ill people there, had not wanted to stay, and had returned home the same evening. This event had the effect of intensifying Juha's aggressive feelings toward hospital institutions, and with a friend he then wrote the story of a patient's case history for one of the big weekly magazines so as to stir up debate and perhaps even to improve the position of future patients. He fantasied that the report would be important in alleviating the hardships of patients even after his death. He had premonitions, though, about the attitude toward him in the hospital after this, and expressed his fear that the article might be disastrous for him. But he had wanted to bring the facts to general notice because throughout his illness he himself had experienced great insecurity and anxiety that were apparently caused by the hospital staff.

Phase III: Approaching the Grief of Loss

Before seeing the patient the next time in the hospital, the therapist received a call from his wife saying that he was so tired and ill that he could not see anyone. When the therapist then did go to see him as agreed, his wife was with him, and this became the first opportunity to get acquainted with her. After a few words had been exchanged, she left the room.

Juha appeared to be very pleased, and experienced the fact that he himself could make the decision about the therapist's coming to see him as something very positive. After a moment of silence the patient began to wonder if he was so mentally ill as to require psychiatric treatment. The therapist once more commented that when one is distressed it is a relief to talk with an outside expert, and that a patient is equally entitled to this. Juha then said that he had begun to fear losing his mind. He spoke of the hallucinations he had had after being admitted to the hospital. One evening before falling asleep he had the sensation that he was reading a book he could not understand at all. When he realized that in fact there was no book, he was frightened. The experience of reading had been very real. Similarly, the day before, when he had had a spell of nausea after the administration of medicine, he had experienced another hallucination that had frightened him still further. He had reached for a receptacle which lay on his bedside table. The cardboard receptacles had stuck together, however, and, not being able to get them apart, he grew very irritated and worried, and finally in a fit of rage had tried to use his teeth as well. At that very moment he had seen right in front of him huge red jaws tearing and wrenching at something. These experiences had been very frightening, and he was anxious and apprehensive about whether this meant that he might "go mad." His mind was put at rest by the therapist's reassuring remark that anyone in a state of fatigue and anxiety can have similar experiences and still not be mentally ill in any way.

Juha now began to express his sorrow about his friends forgetting him so easily: "One is pushed out of everything." He had heard that his colleagues were planning a party in honor of two of them. They had been in the habit of going on binges now and then, and Juha had always enjoyed them. He was sad because his illness would not allow him to participate any more, but he had decided to send a telegram as a token of remembering his friends. He said that he had expected his friends to react somehow and was very disappointed that they had not even made a phone call, because he could have received the call at any time of the day. "I would have acted differently myself, I would have organized a delegation to bring roses even in the middle of the night, confident that the staff would understand and allow it." As a matter of fact, his friends had asked his wife to tell him how grateful they were for the telegram and how they appreciated his gesture, but this did not quite satisfy the patient's regressive expectations. Juha said that he had refused to receive visitors because he did not want anyone to see him in such poor and feeble condition. By accusing his friends he strove to abolish the painful sorrow caused by the loss of them. This incident took place three months before his death.

Juha visited at home for a time, and on his return to the hospital he was tired and dissatisfied. He said his visit home had turned out to be a complete failure, and he had to return earlier than he was due. His mother-in-law had spent the weekend with them, and he had been very much annoyed with her. He was annoyed because there was an outsider in his home when he came for a vacation. Most irritating about the mother-in-law had been the servility she showed on various occasions and her strenuous efforts not to disturb him. He was enraged by the way she silently "crept" around the apartment. Juha would rather have seen her act normally and accept his presence in a natural way. The situation had grown so unbearable that the patient had wanted to return to the hospital early, on Sunday evening. On this occasion, too, the patient suppressed his grief by the mobilization of aggressions.

Juha then began to describe how unsatisfactory his home was. The couple lived in a one-room apartment with kitchenette and bathroom. His wife had never had a flare for housekeeping or making the home cosy. "I have been used to a spacious, beautiful home ever since my childhood, and I long for different surroundings. My wife comes from a more unpretentious home, and perhaps that is the reason she cannot see the importance of a nice, cosy home." To the therapist's inquiry whether they had ever talked the matter over, Juha replied in amazement that "you don't discuss these things." Just before Juha fell ill they had made plans to acquire a bigger apartment in the same building, but nothing had come of it. He now felt content that they had not gone through with the plan, as he became ill.

After this Juha began to speculate about how his wife would manage after his death. They had never discussed the question with each other. The therapist encouraged Juha to take up the subject of his impending death with his wife. Juha said he was quite willing to do so, and then inquired if the therapist could talk with his wife because he thought that his illness was a great strain on her, too. The therapist agreed to see his wife the next day, and so she began her therapy two months before the patient's death. The therapy was continued regularly once a week for about a year after Juha's death.

When the therapist came for the next session after the meeting with his wife, Juha was annoyed with her, demanding to know whether his wife had not called to say that he was in a bad state and had not wanted to see the therapist. His wife arrived at the same time to see him, but Juha told her to go away, and far enough "not to eavesdrop." Juha was in a bad humor, telling the therapist that he was tired and might vomit at any minute. Then his mood changed, and in a conciliatory manner he said he was getting new drugs that caused heart symptoms along with other side effects. He was afraid his heart might not stand the strain, and in a soothing way told the therapist about the good care he was receiving; how well he was looked after; how he had been allowed to read his case reports and a copy of an inquiry about his case sent elsewhere. By trying to calm himself he sought to keep the fear of death out of awareness. He did not want the light to be lit in the room, but wanted to be with the therapist in the dusk. On the therapist's departure he was more serene and content, asking for his wife to be called back.

The story Juha had written had been published in the weekly magazine, and the therapist told him she had read it. He was very pleased by the general interest it had aroused, and told the therapist about the favorable attention paid to him, about the phone calls and letters he had received from other cancer patients. He felt that there was a bond between himself and other cancer patients which lessened his fear of loneliness and his sorrow. After the publication of the article, the doctors caring for him had begun to pay more attention to him, some had become on more friendly terms with him, he had awakened more interest in general, and he felt that he could now pariticpate in his own hospital treatment in a new way.

Phase IV: The Three Last Weeks

Juha's attitude toward his environment gradually became more and more regressed, and he had severe pains, especially in his back. A neurological examination had been performed, and this worried him. He did not take the trouble to hide his aggressive feelings, or his accusations, from the staff. "They continue to disturb me at all hours; even now, during our conversation, they keep running into the room; they wake me up in the middle of the night as soon as I have fallen asleep; they don't give me my medicine on time," and so on. Physically Juha's condition had grown worse. He was very tired, had lost weight, and his color had become yellowish. Psychically he was calm, however, and did not appear to be anxious. He said that he had not been able to sleep for a great many nights. He lay in his bed half dozing, and it became apparent that he stubbornly fought against falling asleep. He was afraid of falling asleep and of dying during his sleep. In order to stay awake he made himself keep his eyes open. He stared in terror at the ceiling and spoke very little. The range of his interest at this time embraced only himself and his hospital room. After a long period of silence, Juha said that he was so tired that he just wanted to pass away in his sleep, that he no longer had the energy to think about recovery, he was simply too tired and fatigued. Then he added that there was so much to be done, that it's not fair to have to die so young. He would have wanted "to spend the summer at his parents' summer cottage, and to row a boat on the lake there."

In this phase of therapy the therapist just sat quietly at the patient's bedside. Juha was able to relax gradually and even dared to doze off for short periods, to wake up again with his eyes round with fear. He found that the therapist's presence gave him a sense of protection against death. This was three weeks before his death. Not until after Juha's death, during the final phase of his wife's therapy, was the fact disclosed that at this very time he had seriously considered committing suicide and had even asked his wife for her consent. His wife had entreated him not to do it for her sake, and Juha had agreed to comply with her wish. Juha never even hinted at this event.

When the therapist next went to see Juha, his wife was there too. Upon entering the room, the therapist heard Juha groan in pain and say that he could not talk or receive anyone because he was so tired. She then left, saying she would come again when he felt he could receive her. At the following therapy appointment, his wife said that Juha had hoped to see the therapist the next day. During the next therapy session Juha was in good spirits, saying that "I have the strength now to be hopeful again, for at last they have found a medicine that takes the pain away." The conversation then rambled on along rather light and inconsistent lines. Juha said he had asked to be allowed a home visit. He exaggerated his strength in a hypomanic manner, belittling the symptoms of weakness. Apprehensive of the regressive dependence on the therapist, he strove to keep her emotionally at a distance. He did not want to make an appointment for the next therapy session, saying his wife could make it for him later. This, then, was to be the last therapeutic meeting with the patient.

Juha died a little over a week later, having spent his last few days at home, in his wife's care. According to the wife, those last days at home had been a good, warm time for them both. Juha had been "happy in her company the whole time." Even the pains that were more constant during the last days could not diminish Juha's pleasure, and the joy of being together had lasted. The evening before his death, Juha had gone to bed at the usual time, and had fallen asleep soon because he was very tired, having been up the night before. After a couple of hours, his wife had been aroused by Juha's difficult breathing, and she saw that he was dying. He was fully conscious during his dying process, and watched his wife make arrangements for transportation to the hospital in a detached way. On and off he had hallucinated about being at a baseball game, and talked enthusiastically about "off side." At times he had also hallucinated about the "christconflict" (a word coined by the patient from Christ and conflict) between him and his mother. He had been content to go back to the hospital, and his wife stayed with him to the end. Just before his death he had asked that they go home, and then he had died peacefully in his wife's arms. He had not been in anguish or fearful, and his wife thought that "Juha had not been aware of the proximity of death." The couple had never discussed his death except when he asked for her consent to commit suicide. Neither had they talked about her future after his death. Yet their relationship was a warm and close one, and the wife felt that both thought about these things,

and that they conveyed their thoughts to each other by
gestures and expressions.

SUMMARY OF THE CASE

The patient was a 30-year-old man who had been taken ill
with carcinoma of the testis. The illness was diagnosed a year
and a half before his death, and he was in psychotherapy for
about six months.

The patient was married but had no children. He had
discontinued his university studies and was employed at the
onset of the illness. His neurotic problems were reflected as
symptoms of the oedipal-phase conflicts manifested mostly in
his relationships with his parents and other figures of authority. He openly hated his father and brother and avoided their
company, but sought the favorite child's position offered by
his mother.

In phase one of the psychotherapy, when the patient had
discovered symptoms of cancer in the enlarged testis, he
feared having contracted a venereal disease or cancer.
Because he was afraid of doctors and medical examinations,
he postponed seeking care for four months. Even before the
illness had been diagnosed the patient had a neurotic fear of
operations and of dying during surgery. His reaction on being
informed of the cancer was to mobilize his hatred of the
doctors who had passed on the information to him, and to
reactivate his adolescent hatred of his father. On the other
hand, there was no evidence of conscious fear of death, nor of
grief or depression. He chose a female psychotherapist and
wanted to secure control of her and the therapy. This phase
of therapy was mainly characterized by the patient's effort to
externalize his strict superego, which relieved his anxiety by
allowing him to experience threatening death mostly as a
neurotic fear. On the other hand, the transference to the
therapist was reinforced by the patient's simultaneous efforts

to describe his good qualities to her, his relationship to his work and colleagues. He experienced that in this striving his ego ideal and thereby his narcissism were supported by the therapist.

In the second phase of therapy, alongside the weakening of his physical condition and the intensifying pains, the patient tried to fend off and to suppress his anxiety and fear of death by using the therapist as his auxiliary ego, by resorting to the use of sedatives prescribed by her, and by memories of therapy sessions in the lonely hours of the night when he could not sleep. He also fantasied that he could now write a book about his life which would serve as an auxiliary ego after his death. He now felt that he could accomplish this task because of the ego support given by the therapist, but time and diminished physical resources were against him.

The fantasy wish to be able to leave a book about himself to the world, and the relinquishing of the wish demanded by reality, the patient experienced as a blow to his self-esteem. In an effort at reparation he turned to reminiscences of his childhood, when his mother had smoothed out the conflicts between him and his father. Regression to the enjoyment of his mother's childhood support, and the experience of the transference to the therapist as a desire to seek motherly protection, frightened the patient. He tried to avoid the experience by fleeing to a sanatorium where, however, he was even more frightened by the sight of weak old people dependent on others. He then gave up the fight against fear and resorted to the therapist's help by asking his wife to call the therapist to visit him because he no longer had the strength to go to see her.

He was now able to use the transference relation as an ego support in reality also, and arrived at a compromise between his expectations and reality. He no longer tried to write a book about himself, but instead, with the aid of a friend, wrote a report for a magazine of the numerous

problems encountered by cancer patients. He accomplished
this as a well neutralized and sublimated task, and in such a
constructive spirit as to secure the support of his surroundings, thereby reinforcing his secondary narcissism and pre-
venting the helpless hatred from taking the upper hand with
regard to his ego functions.

In the third phase of therapy, the patient had grown very
weak, but he still fought against progressing regression with
the fantasy that he had control over the therapist's comings
and goings, and over the therapy itself. The hallucinations he
had in his weakened condition made him afraid of "going
mad" and of losing control over himself. The hallucinations
brought the fears connected with death into the sphere of his
consciousness. These were the fear of not understanding what
was happening to him when he hallucinated reading an
incomprehensible book, and the fear connected with loss of
primary narcissism that was reflected as a hallucination of
"the hungry wolf problem"—the oral fear of a tearing,
wrenching, red jaw. These fears—fear of going mad, fear of
the incomprehensible, fear of losing primary narcissism—
were all combined into the fear of losing ego control over the
drives and thus being overpowered by his own drive impulses.
However, the therapist's ego support sufficed to reinforce the
patient's ego functions, and he then approached the mourning of losses leaning on the transference and the therapeutic
alliance. He grieved over the loss of his friends and his work,
but the loss of his home he approached by subduing his grief
and mobilizing his hatred, which was then aimed at the
disturbing elements—at his mother-in-law and the deficien-
cies of his home. Approaching the grief of losing his wife, the
patient momentarily felt the desire to share the mourning
with her, and he empathically understood that she, too, had
been relieved. Yet the sorrow was too painful for the couple
to verbalize the death or loss of one another. On the contrary,
the grief and the fear of losing his wife led the patient to

make arrangements for her therapy with his own therapist. Thus the therapist became a new version of the patient's auxiliary ego—she would take care of his grieving wife after his death. The patient made plain his ambivalent emotions about his wife's therapy, however: on the one hand, he was calmed by her therapy starting; on the other hand, his feelings of anger were aroused, bringing with them competitive obstacles.

In no phase of therapy did the patient really deeply mourn the oncoming losses caused by death, nor was it possible to perceive any actual mourning going on that would have resulted in introjection of the object and led to adaptation. Instead, the patient used first the therapist and then his wife as an auxiliary ego that lasted until his death. The patient transferred his mother transference from his therapist to his wife after he had made arrangements for her therapy. Having done this he declared his satisfaction because he felt that he was well cared for in the hospital.

In the fourth phase of therapy, during the last three weeks, the patient was at times in anguish because the pains grew worse, but he felt no greater anxiety. The almost constant presence of the therapist and above all of his wife eradicated the fear of loneliness and strengthened the ego defenses against fear of death. This was seen in the fight he put up against sleep in the fear that he might never awaken, after which the presence of the therapist allowed him to fall asleep.

The patient mobilized his libido for the reinforcement of his narcissism, and his interest in the external world dwindled to nothing. He felt great fatigue and wanted only to die in his sleep. His bitterness about the illness and his helplessness sometimes got the upper hand, as when he told his wife that he would commit suicide, but he withdrew the threat for her sake because she pleaded with him.

Finally there came a period of intense intimacy between

the couple when the patient regressed to dependence on his wife without experiencing any more fear about being dependent. He resisted the regressive dependence on his therapist, however, and aggressively pushed her away. After this split of object and emotions, he felt free from the aggressive part of dependence, and ambivalent devotion and libido were then directed at his wife, who was constantly present. He died in the lasting positive intimacy of the two-person relationship, his libido being directed at his wife on the one hand, and, as narcissistic libido, at himself on the other. He died quietly, without preceding unconsciousness and without awareness of dying. His wife was able to retain the intense intimacy of the relationship with her dying husband mainly because she could work through her grief gradually in her own therapy.

CONCLUSIONS AND DISCUSSION OF THE CASES

ON THE TRANSFERENCE OF THE DYING PATIENT

In defense against the fear of the proximity of death, the dying patient resorts first of all to mechanisms of denial and to those ego defenses that in the past he has found reliable in fending off unbearable anxiety. In the absence of the psychotherapeutic transference relationship, the patient's defense mechanisms tend to apply mainly to already existing patterns of rationalization, such as various religious and philosophical rituals and trains of thought that are reflected in ritualized creativity and a diversity of rites. When the two-person transference relationship is available to the patient, patterns of rationalization lose their meaning and the patient works through his dying process as though living in a relationship of two, repetitively experiencing real events of his life's various developmental phases and those significant fantasies he has had of that relationship. When personal creativity is highly developed, the dying person, aided by his creativity, passes through the dying process as the experience of an internalized two-person relationship.

Whenever it is possible to attain a transference in the course of the dying process while both physical and psychic regressions deepen, the mechanisms of denial used as a defense undergo a transformation. In the beginning, denial is more intellectual, more rational, and embraces mainly temporal matters and the progressing illness. On a more regressive ego level denial adopts magic forms, and omnipotent fantasies about the therapist and the self are experienced as reality.

When the transference reaches its optimum, the dying patient is able to experience the grief of losses and the working through of mourning. By means of the two-person relationship the patient can transfer cathexis from the lost object to the transference and thereby maintain his own narcissistic value. It is not possible for anyone to achieve this alone, for in the absence of the transference the dying process takes the form of a series of painful narcissistic humiliations and object losses that are invested with the emotional qualities of exploitation.

In the final stage, death loses its entire meaning for the patient when he experiences his existence as a fusion, as a total union with another person. The dying patient has fantasies of being fused with the therapist, and the outlines of his own ego become diffuse. A comparison can be made to the mother-infant relationship before the first individuation (Mahler, 1968, Chapter 1). The difference is conspicuous, however; a dying patient is ill, anguished, and unhappy, lacking the infant's positive joy in living. For the developing infant the adult with whom he can identify is his auxiliary ego. The dying person, on the other hand, finds in the adult an auxiliary ego that he has invested with the qualities he himself has relinquished. Thus the auxiliary ego of a dying person is mostly a fantasy that will never be fulfilled on the reality level. Only that part of the auxiliary ego that is connected with carrying out some personal wishes of the dying person can become a reality. The intensity and significance of the two-person relationship, however, are equally important in the two cases, and their absence brings about the fixation of the process and the accompanying conflict, anxieties, and symptoms. The process of death must therefore be regarded as a series of events conforming with causality. The process ends in personal death, which has been made conscious on the ego level. The patient's whole life is condensed in the dying process, and he mediates parts of it to other people in the form of the two-person relationship experiences and derivatives thereof, such as creativity.

In all three cases I have presented, the patient's transference to the therapist became very conspicuous, reflecting the intensity of therapy. In all the cases the transference continued positively for most of its duration, and only in the final stage of the death process did the patients direct their aggression at the therapist. The sole content of the aggression was disappointment at the therapist's inability to respond to the patients' omnipotent fantasies, the inability to put a stop to the death process and to offer the patient a ready pattern for dying. Not until all this had been worked through were the patients called Tom and Aino capable of forming a creative transference to the therapist. In these cases the creative interaction comprised the intense feeling of unity the patient had acquired as an extension of his/her mourning work, and finally the internalization of the therapist as the last experience in the transference. This did not take place in the case of Juha, in my opinion because his various difficult neurotic problems from the very beginning were an obstacle to building a positive therapeutic transference, and therefore the ambivalent relationship persisted. For one thing, in terms of time there was no possibility at all of solving his diverse problems. To the end Juha maintained a defensive and mastering transference to his therapist and to his wife, who functioned as bitherapist, and even at best the transference never reached the stage of functioning as a creative two-person relationship. The patient's age was another decisive factor in the transference. He was at the summit of man's life, whereas Tom was a child and Aino an old woman, and for them the two-person relationship and the dependence on another person were natural because of their age. Contracting cancer of the testis in the prime of his life, on top of being childless, was narcissistically a very traumatic experience for Juha, and he approached the sorrow and losses in the manner of a narcissistically traumatized patient, fearing the grief, mobilizing his aggressions to enhance his narcissism, and using the two-person relationship defensively in the service of his narcissism. With the aid of the splitting mechanism he directed his aggression to the therapist, whom he then rejected, and his libido to his wife, whom he experienced as being in his possession to the end.

On the Defensive Organization of the Dying Patient

In the dying patient a strong, multiple defense organization in accordance with van der Leeuw's (1958) definition can be observed in addition to the individual ego defense mechanisms. Besides the person's use of characteristic defense mechanisms and personal defensive organization against fear of death, the earliest ego defenses against anxiety also play an important part in the process. These are denial, projection, splitting, and introjection in their archaic forms.

During the dying process the patient defends himself not only against the separation fear of the various psychosexual developmental phases and the fear of annihilation, but also against the unknown and the nonbeing. Death is experienced as castration in a broad sense when defense against fear of death is defense against the castration fear of each psychosexual developmental phase. Defense against fear of death is built up as though the person were defending himself against the castration fear of the oedipal, anal, and oral phases. In addition, fear of death can be experienced as fear of losing personal structures; as the fear of loss of superego, loss of love of ego ideal; as fear of loss of ego skills and loss of ego control; and finally, as fear of being overwhelmed by drive impulses without any possibility of directing them at any object, and fear of becoming the object of one's own aggressive impulses.

Unknown death, in the meaning of not having been experienced before, lies outside the sphere of human comprehension. When death has the implication of the unknown, one cannot defend oneself against it without transforming the unknown into something one knows by investing it with familiar features. For this reason death acquires its peculiar threat on each psychosexual developmental level. Fear of death is endowed with typical individual features according to personal development, traumas, and internal and external events and object relations that have formed the individual's personality. Similarly, developmental stages or specific personality structures affect defense against fear of death, as happened in Juha's case. He experienced fear of death as the strong fear of castration of the oedipal phase, and consequently identified with the castrater as a means of defense. In addition, he experienced death as a threat by the superego, and therefore strove to externalize his superego. Later on, he experienced death as a threat of the drives to the ego. Drive impulses as such and the drivelike quality of the superego had interfered with his object relations and his possibility of attaining gratification in an intimate two-person relationship because of the complexity of his neurotic problems. During his dying process he experienced fear of death only as an extended neurotic fear, and he sought to defend himself mainly by the control of external objects.

Among the means of defense against castration fear in the oedipal phase are, e.g., the phallic-narcissistic ones. The phallic defensive organization against fear of death was manifested as an intermediary phase in the cases of Tom (Phase II) and Aino (Phase III), as well as in the poetry of Edith Södergran (The Saint George Period). They all experienced death as a phallic-narcissistic threat and sought to overcome phallic death by their own even greater phallicity, or to seduce it by feminine-phallic means. The phallic threat was experienced as a strain and a fearful event, and the therapist was also seen as a phallic threat or as a phallic seducer. It was a narcissistic defensive organization devoid of the ego-supportive interaction of the two-person relationship and without the creativity built on that relationship. The phallic defensive organization against death reflects the ambivalence of the three-person relationship of the oedipal phase when the patient's introjected fantasy of phallic threat, phallic rival, or phallic power is intensely in the foreground and thus has acquired the meaning of threatening death. I believe that, from this viewpoint, phallic defensive organization is part of the denial of the real threatening death. These patients strove to deny the true meaning of death as loss of themselves and as loss of their bodies *in toto* by the phallic fantasy of death as only the loss of part of the body or part of the self, in the same way as phallic castration fear is experienced. Thus emphasizing the phallic-narcissistic value of the self seemed rational and provided an enduring defensive organization until it was no longer possible to deny the reality of the illness and the continual deterioration of the psychophysical state by taking flight in a delusion of psychotic regression. Then the phallic defensive organization was broken and the patient needed to find a more real and more enduring protection against death.

A more real and enduring protection against fear of death, in my opinion, is the two-person relationship as such, as an earlier internalized object relation or as the therapeutic two-person relationship with the possibility of transference. In the two-person relationship, on the one hand, the genital inner space features and their sublimated creative forms of the mother-child relationship are emphasized. On the other hand, the regressive efforts of the anal and oral psychosexual developmental phases seek defense against the fear of loss of object and loss of gratification. All in all, there follows the enhancement and accentuation of both the interaction of the early mother-child relationship and the defense mechanisms that have formed, preserved, and reinforced the patient's primary narcissism. In fact, here is to be found the core of my study: in the two-person relationship in the course of the regression of the dying process, *a point is reached where either creativity or the defensive organization becomes the predominant ego function* in the progressing death process. While creativity in mourning is based on the mutual creative illusion of the two-person relationship of Winnicott's transitional phase, the defensive organization against mourning is directed at the control of objects and the individual's own anxiety, and at the acquisition of power. When the defensive organization is predominant in the dying process, the patient strives in the regressive two-person relationship to attain power, to control; to spoil the object by means of anal-sadistic mechanisms; to seize the object by oral-sadistic mechanisms, to devour the object or parts of it; or he will refuse to accept anything at all. When the therapist supports or reinforces the dying patient's primary narcissism by means of the mutual creative illusion, the defense mechanisms are not needed, and development takes the direction of creative communication. This, of course, does not take place if the patient feels himself rejected, worthless, or lonely. The shift from defensiveness toward creativity presupposes that the "healthy omnipotence" of the patient's primary narcissism, and therefore his trust in the therapist's good will, have remained intact, as in the cases of Tom and Aino. Contrarily, Juha's narcissistic deficiency or his so-called "hungry-wolf problem" did not allow the formation of adequate trust in the therapist, but instead compelled him to strive to the end to preserve the problem of dying as the fear of the oedipal phase, and to control his therapist.

In the experiential sense, dying is a different event when it is the result of a mainly defensive organization than when it gradually develops as the result of a creative therapeutic relationship. In my opinion, mainly defensive fantasies of death were discernible in the five patients who met their deaths without intensive psychotherapy and the transference of the two-person relationship (see Chapter 1). As a result of interrupted mourning work, they formed strongly cathected fantasies of existence after death. They transferred their object cathexes at least partly to fantasies of death, and experienced that they were going to meet mother, spouse, or deity in death. Preserving the defensive fantasies was possible only through the ego mechanism of splitting the feelings and/or the object; derivatives of hatred were directed toward the objects they were leaving. In the intensive therapy cases, there was no evidence whatever of splitting in Tom and Aino, and it was very faint in Juha; nor could one perceive strongly cathected fantasies of life after death. The immense anguish, the anxiety, and the death struggle for the "attainment of peace" that precede splitting were present only in the cases in which death came without an intense therapeutic relationship, and in which object cathexes were shifted to fantasies of life after death.

On the Creativity of the Dying Patient

When dying is conceived not according to a variety of rationalization patterns, not as phallic-narcissistic castration, nor as a state of nonbeing not known before, it is experienced as the fear of loss of the childhood two-person relationship. Freud (1926a) and Waelder (1960) established that the separation of an infant from the mother and mother's love gives rise to separation anxiety, which later manifests itself in the fear of death. Winnicott (1974) on his part says that "phenomenal death" that happened to the patient but that the patient was not mature enough to experience has the meaning of "annihilation." According to this conception, fear of death is the childhood fear of total annihilation that has not taken place but threatens to do so now. Winnicott lists the primitive terrors as follows: (1) a return to an unintegrated state; (2) falling forever; (3) loss of psychosomatic collusion, failure of indwelling; (4) loss of sense of real; (5) loss of capacity to relate to objects.

As the dying process proceeds to the regressed level at which the above fears are felt to be real, the creativity of the two-person relationship becomes most significant to the dying person. In itself, dying is of course an entirely personal experience. The therapist cannot participate in the patient's dying process on the psychophysical level, but the dying patient and the therapist together can form a creative interaction, with accompanying creative illusions for the patient to internalize in the mutual relationship, after which dying takes place free from the childhood fears that tend to become activated during the process. Of the patients I studied this was most clearly to be seen in Aino. Her creative ability was highly developed and she was also able to use it during her dying process.

To be able to resort to creativity in the face of separation and threatening death the patient must, I believe, have internalized the interaction of a sufficiently good childhood two-person relationship, and have the additional possibility of forming a therapeutic transference. He is then able to externalize onto the therapist the image internalized in childhood. Thereafter he can again make use of the interaction of the mother-child relationship against the fear of destruction when his own ego functions weaken during the dying process, or when death appears to threaten his primary narcissism. This is not to be regarded as a defensive image that has replaced reality; in other words, it is not an image of existence in which object cathexis could remain intact. The creative illusion based on the mother-child relationship is a part of reality the person has been able to use from infancy onward whenever losses or sorrow have come his way. Above all, the creative illusion has great significance when the patient mourns and loses all object cathexes during the dying process. In the dying process sharing the creative illusion as an experienced reality enables the person to withdraw all object cathexes, even though they are not reattached to other real objects with the ensuing drive gratification. Instead the dying patient forms a creative and mutually shared illusion with the therapist on the basis of childhood experiences. Object cathexis can be shifted to this creative illusion during mourning work. Thus creativity may become an extension of well-accomplished mourning work at the end of the dying process.

It is possible to use creativity as part and extension of mourning work even in the earlier stages of mourning. Creativity in mourning work has great significance for the dying patient, in the form of the auxiliary ego he creates to preserve his personal characteristics after his death. As an auxiliary ego a created product is different from the utilization of a certain person and that person's abilities. In the latter case, the chosen auxiliary ego is invested with ego features of the dying person in the anticipation that those features and duties will be carried on after one's death. The existence of such an auxiliary ego enables the patient to decathect his objects and to leave unaccomplished tasks to the world he is departing. A creative product acting as an auxiliary ego is different. Something even more personal is invested in it than in a person functioning as an auxiliary ego. A created product has a stronger narcissistic cathexis than can be contained in any other form of activity. The dying person can invest the products of his creativity with features and parts of his narcissism and then experience as a reality that these products will survive in the world after his death.

Either a person or a created product, or both, had been perceptibly adopted as an auxiliary ego by all the patients I studied, disregarding their ability to form a therapeutic transference or not. Creativity as an auxiliary ego during the dying process was conspicuous in the life of the artistically talented Edith Södergran, and her poetry reflects the interaction of the two-person relationship as strikingly as if it had been experienced in a transference. The impression that lingers in her poetry is that she was able to use her talent in the course of the long mourning and dying process, and even in the various phases of regression, because of the internalized two-person relationship. The poems reflecting the various phases of mourning and creativity were not autistic writings nor purely narcissistic expressions; rather, by creative means she preserved in them the interaction of the two-person relationship for the world to behold. Aino used the "Mimosa" poem in a similar way. Tom's stamp collection and his bird picture were creative products with the function of auxiliary egos, and he invested them with an abundance of shared illusions of creativity. All three had fantasies of the joy and appreciation the recipients would experience, and all experienced that features of their own personal human relations were preserved in the created products.

Perhaps creativity is the only means of transferring one's own narcissistic features to another person, not only in the course of the dying process, but in general. Narcissism as such cannot survive after the patient's death. Primary narcissism is built on the good interaction of the early two-person relationship, and the interaction can be mediated by the developed means of creativity or by the shared creative illusion with another person, along with the features of personal narcissism. Creative interaction in itself does not incite feelings of envy in the recipient, nor the desire to use defense, as can easily happen when narcissism and self-esteem are emphasized by other means (see Chapter 5). Creativity is experienced as a worthy gift from one person to another, and creativity is experienced by the dying person as the greatest and final gift he can bestow before dying and relinquishing life. The last experience in the psychotherapy of the dying patient concerns this "gift." During the treatment of Tom (Phase III) I was unable to receive the "gift," because it incited guilt, as the therapist's countertransference, about the dying person's libidinally giving everything to another. In the case of Aino countertransference was not an obstacle, and in the "gift" of her narcissism lay the interaction that contained the emotional reality of the shared illusion of the two-person relationship, which was of great help to Aino in her death.

PART IV

Summary and General Discussion

8.

Summary

PART I

A Review of the Literature

The psychoanalytic approach to the understanding of death is based on the assumption that death as the absolute end of life is inconceivable to the human mind. We are able to investigate and to understand the fantasies that accompany death, the chains of thought and emotional reactions aroused by the realization that death signifies being dead, when we look at them as man's effort to bridge the gap that he cannot explain in terms of causality and determinism or feel in terms of experience. Freud's view was that fundamentally man does not believe in his own death: "... the man of prehistoric times survives unchanged in our unconscious. Our unconscious, then, does not believe in its own death; it behaves as if it were immortal" (1915, p. 296). Klein (1948) on her part believed that there is an unconscious knowledge that death means a total end, and Jaques (1965) claimed that the unconscious contains experiences that may later on equal conscious perception of death.

A neurotic fear of death has no connection with actual physical death; rather, the neurotic conception of death is symbolic of earlier separation anxieties (Fenichel, 1945; Hinton, 1967; Stekel, 1927-1928; Verwoert and Elmore,

1967). Adaptation to death is related to the person's maturation and to the various phases of crisis in his life, and is
different at the various ages — childhood, adolescence, mid-
life, and old age (Alexander and Adelstein, 1965; Easson,
1968; A. Freud, 1960, 1967; Hinton, 1967; Jaques, 1965;
Stern, 1968).

Fantasies of death fill the blank that this unknown condition leaves in our minds. In these fantasies death can be
represented as a continuation of life in some other form
(Hinton, 1967), or as punishment or reward for a morally
bad or good life (Feifel, 1959; Stokes, 1966), or it can be
personified in the shape of an animal or a man (Kemppinen,
1967) or a threatening father figure (McClelland, 1964).
Fantasies of death may take a pleading form, or be representative of a return to the frustration-free intrauterine state,
or be personifed as the seducer (Bromberg and Schilder,
1936), or they can have the meaning of reunion with the lost
object, dead parent, spouse, etc. (Freud, 1926a; Eissler,
1955; Waelder, 1960; Greenberger, 1965).

When the person is faced with the reality of meeting
death in the immediate future, he undergoes a series of
changes. These changes have been illustrated by the case
reports of Felix Deutsch (1935), Eissler (1955), Sandford
(1957), Joseph (1962), and Norton (1963). Protection against
threatening death is sought by utilization of all the ego
defenses, foremost among them being the mechanism of
denial. When the mechanism of denial diminishes, the
mourning process begins with the mourning work. The dying
person then relinquishes his objects, his life, and his body by
way of mourning, while simultaneously the wish for the
immortality of his own personality leads to the formation of
the "auxiliary ego" to maintain his object relations after his
death, or he envisions life continuing in his children, his
work, or his accomplishments. As the death process progresses and regression deepens, a phase often follows when by

means of the splitting mechanism the dying person divides his emotions and his objects into two — bad and good. The world to be left is considered bad, while fantasies of death or fantasies of oneness with the therapist or any other human being who has stood by him are good.

THE PRESENT CLINICAL STUDY

The material comprises five subjects, two males and three females, of the ages 69, 71, 79, 36, and 83 years, all of whom died of some form of cancer. Psychotherapeutic sessions were held with them for one to three months until their deaths. This study was an introduction to the psychodynamics of the dying patient as it is reflected in the two-person relationship, but it was not psychoanalysis proper with a coherent trans- ference, as my later studies have been (see Part III). The subjects under study differed in their personal problems, in their personality structures, and in their social standing. Observation of the dying process in this study, and in my later studies as well, had the purpose of focusing attention on the changes taking place in the patient without comparisons to other patients, and of acknowledging that the same specific feature could be differently determined in each individual case.

All the patients denied death as an absolute end to life, either by means of a fantasy conforming to some religious pattern or by the belief that they would be reunited with already dead relatives after death. At times they were afraid of death, and at times they believed that death was a good and safe existence. The only patient in the reproductive age for short periods eroticized her fantasy of death.

The main defense mechanism against fear of death was denial of varying degree and varying content. As denial gradually lost its protective power during the progressing dying process, grief reactions and mourning work began. The libidinal cathexis released in the mourning work was shifted mainly to fantasies of existence after death, but in part also to the people caring for the patient and in part to the therapist. In some cases, introjection of the therapist manifested itself as an experience of having him accompany the patient in death as a defense against the fear of separation.

WOMAN AND CREATIVITY

When the traditional and generally accepted part of the culture and the personal contribution of the individual meet in art and in science, the traditional part is transformed and recreated (Milner, 1957; Modell, 1970). There are two main lines to be noted in creative activity. One denotes grandeur, force, power, striking force, etc., and utilizes phallic symbols. The other is indicative of mutuality, intimacy, care, warmth, etc., utilizing the symbols of what Erikson (1951, 1968) has called the woman's inner space. The unique features of woman's creativity relate to her biological constitution (Greenacre, 1960; Erikson, 1968; Winnicott, 1971), although the significance of bisexual identification is outstanding in all creative activity (Winnicott, 1971).

MOURNING WORK IN POETRY

The description of the mourning work of the Finnish poetess, Edith Sòdergran, is based on her poetry and her biography. She died, after a protracted dying process, of pulmonary tuberculosis. Her father had died of the same disease, and the sorrowful longing and loneliness she felt after his death were reflected in her "schoolgirl poetry." She identified with the dead father, and a strong object cathexis to the father stayed permanently in her unconscious fantasies. She did not have the capacity to transfer the cathexis to another object by means of mourning. This may possibly have been an additional influence in her contracting the very same disease, pulmonary tuberculosis. She experienced the disease in the lungs as an impregnation; she had been impregnated by death. Fantasies of death and the oedipal object became eroticized, and the disease was symbolic of a child in woman's inner space.

In the process of Edith Södergran's illness and death three separate phases can be distinguished regarding the working through of sorrow. After a lyrical, peaceful time immediately after the onset of the illness, there followed a phase of massive denial of fear of death and death's proximity, "The Joyous Year." Although she trusted her own capacity to appease and seduce the harsh death, in her tranquil, solitary moments she yearned for the protection of the preoedipal two-person relationship. In her struggle with death during the Saint George period she took refuge in strongly phallic fantasies until at last this defense diminished, and in the last three years she became absorbed in experiences of symbiotic protection and creative mutuality in her poetry. Owing to her creative potential, and with the support of earlier internalized objects, she was able to work through the mourning process and the mourning work productively without a psychotherapeutic transference relationship.

PART II

Mourning and Narcissism

Taking Freud's (1917) basic conceptions for the psychoanalytic understanding of grief, and his idea of the shifting of object cathexis (1923) as a starting point, the mourning process can be considered in a broad sense as an important and universal means of reaction to adaptation and growth that always includes the loss of something old while a new structure is built. Optimal progress of the mourning process

(Pollock, 1961) requires a good internalized object and/or a good external object. Instead of a good object, narcissistic persons have early fantasies of a grandiose self and/or over-valued narcissistically cathected objects (Kohut, 1971; Kern-berg, 1974). A narcissistic person experiences the mourning process as something unreasonable; for him sorrow has the meaning of unbearable anxiety. His defense against mourn-ing is found in strong measures that are phallic-narcissistic in nature.

PHALLICITY AS A DEFENSE

Phallicity is presented in this study as a defensive organi-zation against the fear of loneliness and separation, the fear of the unknown, and inner space envy, all of which can take the form of castration fear. Phallic is not the equivalent of masculine, nor is its opposite feminine. The opposite of phallic is castrated (Freud, 1908b, 1924, 1926a). Phallic omnipotence arises when the child transfers the omnipotent fantasies of the symbiotic unity of the mother-child relation-ship to the phallus. After this the child is as omnipotent in his fantasies in his relation to the phallus as he earlier was in his symbiotic relation to the mother. Phallic fantasies are a safeguard against frustrations in the interaction of human relations, and actually are the consequence of, or lead to, poor capacity to utilize other people as objects.

When development is optimal, a little boy, too, can resolve mother envy without resorting too much to the phallic defensive organization, by means of identification with the sublimated forms of woman's inner space features.

The forerunners of woman's genital inner space are the oral and the anal inner spaces. The mutually shared illusion of the transitional phase of the mother-child relationship (Winnicott, 1953) endows the child with the capacity to adopt those inner space features that lead to adult genitality and generativity through experiences of the gradually improving creativity of the two-person relationship. Whatever the child is unable to share with his mother physically, he can share verbally by means of the mutual creative illusion, through experiencing the mother's inner space features. Against the part of the mother's sexuality that remains unclear in the child's mind, he finds defense in phallic fantasies.

MOURNING AND CREATIVITY

Creativity is an ego function different from and in many respects opposite to the ego defense mechanisms. In the fields of art and science creativity is among the goals that are narcissistic, ambitious, and utilitarian. Creativity has an important role in human relations and in the mourning process. In Winnicott's terms (1971) creativity is a "thing in itself," and the illusion of the transitional object of the transitional phase (Winnicott, 1953) is the child's first creative attitude toward the environment. The capacity internalized in the transitional phase can be the foundation for a creative attitude toward other people and toward animate and inanimate nature. Besides the transitional phase illusion, creativity contains the sublimated inner space features of motherhood and, furthermore, it contains as one component the identification with the active mother who produces from her inner space. Creativity is thus also a solution for motherhood envy.

According to the conception presented here, mourning work and creativity are complementary to each other, and creativity is a continuation of mourning. By creating something new and unprecedented, creativity has greater scope than does adaptation to changed circumstances in mourning work. When, on the other hand, creativity replaces mourning, it is manifested in compulsive repetition. Phallic illusion is not creative in the same sense as creativity, which develops from the illusion of the transitional phase. Neither is it a continuation of mourning, which it tends to obstruct, but is a defense against the painful sorrow of the mourning process.

PART III

THE DYING CHILD

As discussed in the psychoanalytic literature, mourning reactions and primitive or more developed mourning work with changes in object cathexis are to be seen in children only after object constancy has been achieved (A. Freud, 1952; Nagera, 1970; Furman, 1964a; Wolfenstein, 1965, 1966). The child's capacity to mourn depends not only on developmental stage but also on environmental factors (Nagera, 1970), on the parent or parent substitutes who function as the child's ego support (Nagera, 1970; A. Freud, 1960; Shambaugh, 1961; Furman, 1964b). The psychoanalytic literature does not contain previous presentations of psychoanalytic studies of a child's reactions to his own death and the consequent mourning work.

The dying process of a 12-year-old boy with leukemia is described. During the last year and three months of his life he was in psychoanalytic psychotherapy. He formed a coherent transference to his therapist, and the dying process was reflected in the transference. He externalized his superego to the environment and the therapist, and the dreaded death acquired phallic and phallic-magical features. His defense against these features was in the fantasies of his own even greater phallic-magical ability. He tried to avoid death by means of a substitute sufferer.

Having perceived that death was unavoidable, he sought for ego support in the creative interaction with the therapist and the bitherapist. His trust in the creative means and in the creative interaction with another person in fending off the fears and anxiety inherent in death was reflected in his auxiliary egos and in the therapeutic relationship. He worked through mourning in the therapeutic relationship and regressed to a symbiotic intimacy with the therapist. He died supported by the symbiotic protection. At the end of the dying process, he had no fantasies of going to another place waiting for him, and therefore his libido was invested in those who took care of him.

Two Dying Adults

A common observation in the literature has been that the formation of an intense two-person relationship with a dying adult meets with great difficulty. Eissler (1955) refers to the difficulty encountered by the therapist in his endeavors to understand the dying empathically and to identify with him, because of the underlying fear of being himself drawn into the process. Of course, no one can work through his own death in advance. In all presentations of case histories of dying patients emphasis is laid on the prime importance of the patient's transference to the therapist in psychotherapy.

Two cases are presented: a female, aged 65, who died of cancer of the ventricle, and a male, aged 30, who died of carcinoma of the testis. The female patient was in intensive analytic psychotherapy for one year and three months, and the male in dynamic-supportive psychotherapy for six months, both until their deaths.

From the very beginning, the woman was able to form a coherent and positive transference to the therapist, reflecting the wish to defend against fear of death by means of strong idealization that denied the existence of envy and rivalry in her world. She wanted to govern the frightening death through her own goodness. Later on the defense took feminine-phallic form, and she sought external phallic protection against death, which she experienced as phallic. After with-drawal of denial and the realization that impending death was inescapable, creativity and creative interaction became for her, too, the most important means of protection in the face of the isolation and incomprehensibility of death. The creative interaction within the psychotherapeutic setting was in her case very intense and enriching.

Even her creative ability, which was well sublimated and developed, changed in the course of regression into a more regressed kind of mutual relationship that nevertheless re-tained the creative interaction. Her fear and her inability to comprehend death were intermingled with childhood fears and with the inconceivable mystery of the sexual organs. Finally, she regressed to complete dependence on those caring for her, and externalized on them and on her therapist features of her mother as she had experienced them in the creative interaction. She experienced death as a regressive mutual relationship with all these people.

The man, still in his procreative years, formed a very ambivalent and incoherent transference to his therapist. His diverse neurotic problems and accompanying castration anxiety played a dominant role throughout the dying process. In the final phase he fled from the therapeutic relationship, taking refuge in his wife, and tried to create a fantasy of death in which he governed death as he governed his human relations. His fears—fear of going mad, fear of the inconceiv-able, fear of loss of self—were all merged into the fear of losing ego control over drive impulses. He leaned mainly on defensive solutions even after the realization that death was inescapable. Only occasionally and briefly was he able to lean on the creative interaction of the two-person relationship. The absence of fully developed mourning work, and also of the creativity of the two-person relationship, led to ever more intense defense and isolation as regression deepened. He finally resolved his ambivalence by means of the splitting mechanism, and died in his sleep without being aware of dying.

Conclusions

The main features of the dying process were either defensive or creative. The creative dying process required a good internalized two-person relationship, and this had its origin in the early human relations and/or was formed and internalized in the course of the psychotherapeutic relationship.

In their deaths, the patients resorted to defense not only against the separation fear of the various psychosexual developmental stages and against the fear of annihilation, but also against the unknown and the not-being. The defensive solution of the fear of death utilized the intricate defense organization in which phallicity and phallic-narcissistic defense were dominant. The last defense before death, in order to attain peace, was the splitting of feelings and of object. This was preceded by an intense struggle, by extreme anxiety and anguish.

In the creative two-person relationship, fear of death and death itself were approached as "phenomenal death" connected with early childhood events, as presented by Winnicott (1974). The creative two-person relationship was not a defensive fantasy that could replace reality; on the contrary, it was a creative, shared illusion as a reality of emotion springing from the child's transitional phase. Those patients who had the capacity to seek support in this illusion died in symbiotic intimacy and creative interaction, consciously aware of the proximity of death.

The person's own created product as an auxiliary ego was of great significance in the dying process. It was a means for the dying person to mediate his narcissistic features to the afterworld.

9.

General Discussion

In this study I have looked for answers to some specific questions and have also tried to answer my working hypotheses a.-d.

Hypotheses a. ("The phallic fantasies and the phallic-narcissistic defense organization are part of the denial of fear of death and fear of mourning") and b. ("Phallicity, instead of leading to productive mourning work, obstructs it. It is not endurable as the dying process proceeds either, for the fear of loneliness and the fear of annihilation behind the phallic defense, and the accompanying anxiety and horror, sooner or later overwhelm the dying patient") I believe are valid. These fantasies and defense organization develop at a time when the child's knowledge of and capacity for understanding the mysteries of his parents' genitals, birth of new life, and death, are very limited, but his curiosity about and interest in these very matters are very great.

Against the fear and anxiety of ignorance, the child forms conceptions of his own about sexuality and death in those areas that remain unknown to him. Fear of death and of the mother's genital inner space are invested with phallic-magical features by the child's magical fantasies of the mother and by the symbiotic tie between them in this phase of the child's development. Fear of death and fear of the mother's inner space are fused in the child's mind into the fear of loss of the

232

mother or loss of the self and exclusion from unity with the mother. The phase of development when the child loses the symbiotic mother and gradually acquires the oedipal mother includes the death of the first mother image and the appearance of the mysterious genitals of the second mother image. The child denies his fear by means of his phallic fantasies, and in his fantasy he is then master of both sexuality and the fear of death. In fantasy he forms a relation to his phallus, which, like a magic wand, helps him to transform dreaded things, including the fear of death, into familiar and controllable ones.

As far as I can see, phallicity does not protect the dying patient against the proximity of death; it protects only against the *fear of death*. Understanding death and dying as irreversible and inescapable becomes possible only after a long period of development. Fear of death, when death is feared not because it threatens the child but because of its mysterious and inconceivable nature, already exists at a very early stage of the child's development. The mighty magic wand, the phallus, has been erected as a defense against this fear.

In the dying process phallic defense suffices until the dying person perceives death as an inescapable reality in the near future, or until the fear of death in the distant future is transformed into fear of death in the immediate future. Sometimes it is a painful, difficult, and solitary event because belief in phallic fantasies does not allow the person to seek support in human relations in the face of threatening death.

I am inclined to think that phallic defense, besides being the person's inner conception in the foregoing manner, is firmly sustained by Western culture as a means of defense, specifically as a defense against the fear and the threat of death. Members of this culture tend to turn their backs, or evade the issue in some other way, when a dying person verbalizes his longing, his grief, or his need to have another human being truly near. Our culture does not integrate the emotions that death incites in the human being with the expression of these emotions in the interaction of human relations; instead, it fosters denial by technical, religious, intellectual-phallic, and other phallic defense mechanisms.

When a child or an adult refrains from expressing the true feelings aroused by death and instead keeps them to himself, bravely, aggressively, and phallicly denying the fear of death and relying only on himself, he is rewarded emotionally. It is possible that a different kind of cultural attitude toward the proximity of death could lessen the need of the dying person to mold the dying process mainly by phallic-narcissistic means.

Hypotheses c. ("Instead, creativity based on the two-person relationship provides the patient with a solution and lasting relief in the course of the difficult dying process") and d. ("This kind of creativity can be released for utilization according to the patient's personal abilities in transference, either in the form of creative illusion or of creative activity") state that an alternative resolution and protection as a reality *in the face of death* is offered by the creativity developed in the transitional phase (Winnicott) and the shared illusion of the two-person relationship. This creativity has developed during the entire lifetime into an ever better capacity to avoid loneliness, and into the ability to use the object in a preserving, creative way. In the psychotherapy of the dying patient, creative interaction and creativity are at first present in the form of a more developed, sublimated relationship to the therapist, and then, at the end of the dying process, the creativity of the regressive mother-child relationship prevails.

Not even the regressive, creative interaction is similar to the early mother-child relationship because, for one thing, the dying person at least partly retains the more developed creative ego functions. He mediates creative illusions to the therapist in speech, by expressions and gestures, and he is the partner in whom illusions are born and who brings them into the sphere of the creative interaction. Fear of loneliness disappears when the proximity of death becomes the mutual illusion of the patient and the therapist as an emotional reality in the manner of the transitional phase illusion. For that very reason an event as personal as one's own death can be mediated to and shared with another, the therapist. The experience of the dying patient that even death is shared with the therapist may be understood in this light. It is not a defensive hallucination or psychotic episode. It can be speculated that introjection of the creative interaction between the dying person and the therapeutically oriented therapist as an experience continuing in death is the most highly developed form of mutual experience. It can be the most highly developed because the experiences of the dying person's whole lifetime have accumulated into the capacity to utilize even the very last human relation in a creative and preserving way.

PART V

On the Psychoanalytic Study of Dying

10.

Some Viewpoints on the Phenomenon of Dying

As far as I can see, neither life nor death can be explained or described as a *phenomenon* in psychoanalytic terms. As phenomena they seem more properly to belong in the sphere of biology, philosophy, and/or theology, whereas the hermeneutic-emancipatory scientific values of psychoanalysis lean on the findings revealed by research on the psychic interaction between people as well as the individual's intrapsychic world of experience and thinking. The fundamental aim of psychoanalysis is to develop and increase consciousness, self-awareness, and self-reflection. Despite the fact that a more developed capacity for self-reflection can lead to greater mental health and a more stable state of mind, "health," as for instance Lesche and Stjernholm-Madsen (1976) explain the concept, is not the foremost aim of pure psychoanalysis, in contrast to the many forms of psychotherapy. Nevertheless, the research findings and the frame of reference of psychoanalysis are usable in different modes of psychotherapy oriented toward technical know-how and the manipulatory goal of transforming man to conform to whatever are the current health ideals. Psychoanalytic self-reflection concerning one's *own* life or death can, therefore, be one of the objects of psychoanalysis regardless of the fact that in dying the state of health is severely shaken and the end is inevitable.

239

THE LIFE INSTINCT AND THE
DEATH INSTINCT AS PRINCIPLES

Although Freud's writings cover both psychoanalysis and biology, he was never of a mind to allow biological speculations to lead the way unless he could find a psychoanalytic application for the biological pattern. In his writings of 1920 and 1923 he developed conceptions of the life instinct and the death instinct, Eros and Thanatos, that were based on the physiological processes of anabolism and catabolism. As *principles of the psyche,* the life instinct tends to promote new individual growth and the death instinct tends to destroy and disintegrate already formed individual structures. The life instinct and the death instinct are constantly active and present, and the individual life is a fusion of these two instincts.

Eissler (1972) contends that Ehrenberg's *biological principle* is based on a general principle, formulated by the biologist Karl Ernst von Baer, that " 'The developmental history of the individual is the history of its growing individuality in every respect' " (p. 31), and that " 'Life is marked by the transition from a more or less open system to a more or less closed one' " (p. 32). Ehrenberg's biological principle leads Eissler to draw the conclusion that it is "a biological demonstration of Freud's psychological theory," and that "The biological forces responsible for the transformation of the organism into a closed system are the equivalent of Freud's death drive" (p. 33).

With this in mind, conclusions drawn from the principles of the life and death instincts would indicate that the life instinct is in constant pursuit of new forms by means of extending and liberating individual life patterns, whereas the death instinct strives to overthrow open structures in order to close them into more strictly individual structures. With the aging process man's physiological and psychic structures are gradually shattered, and ultimately new ones are no longer constructed. Then comes the end, the death of the individual. Individual accomplishments, such as offspring and the fruits of labor, are the results of individual and personal enterprise, but they have now been transferred from the sphere of individual structures to the structures of the common culture. In this way the continuous and recurrent disintegration of individual structures, and finally the death of the individual, enrich the common culture. In this sense the individual death instinct can be looked on as a foundation for the wider common culture, and its importance as part of growth and development can be acknowledged.

ON OBJECT CATHEXES

While instincts as such cannot be observed, their various derivatives can be. These derivatives are manifested in the different forms of cathexes as emotional charges, such as interest, thoughts, etc., that are all concerned with the individual himself or with objects that are important to him. Controlled by instincts, the cathexes manifest themselves as the desire to love and to retain the object, or as the urgent drive to hate and to destroy the object. Clinically, instincts are manifested as libido or attachment and as destrudo or aggression, and they can be subjected to psychoanalytic study as principles, unlike the life and death instincts, which elude such study.

For the most part cathexes conform to biological patterns, probably because during his life span the person has cathected different biological incidents in himself, in his parents, and in the general process of growth. Physical growth and the cyclic functions of the human body can be mentioned as examples of these cathexes. The biological pattern of growth has a very strong cathexis, evidenced in the fact that psychic growth follows the biological example. In this way the cathexis of biological processes forms a link between biological and psychic growth.

The libido of the life instinct and the destrudo of the death instinct alternate in both biological and psychic growth. For instance, a child attaches his libido and aggression ambivalently to the parent in the ongoing developmental phase. During each phase libido is prominent as long as the child needs the parent image of that specific developmental phase. When the libidinal cathexis is withdrawn from the parent image, the ambivalent aggressive cathexis takes over and causes the destruction of the useless parent image that the child no longer needs in the next stage of development (Hägglund, 1977).

A precondition for psychic growth is the detachment of libido from objects of the past, sometimes even objects of the present, and, in consequence, its attachment to new objects or recently discovered features of old objects. Psychic growth and creativity have a constant inclination toward new goals and new libidinal aims, although creativity has its own specific features as well. The drivelike attachment of libido to the object is preceded by lust and the desire for gratification. When creativity is guided toward the next phase of development or toward any unknown goal, it is preceded by creative fantasies and the wish to experiment with new solutions.

THE DEATH PROCESS COINCIDES
WITH THE PATTERN OF GROWTH

As far as I can see, the death process is coincident with the pattern of growth as described in the foregoing. In optimal conditions, when past experience has provided enough trust in important human relations in general and consequently also in the therapist, the dying can take refuge in the person caring for him, and together with him pass through the last event of growth, that of dying. If the dying person is isolated or left alone, passing through the death process may be too overwhelming to be experienced as growth, and the experience then becomes one of great anxiety and exploitation, with the realization of the losses and the surrenders when accompanied by progressing psychic regression.

When dying *corresponds to the experience of growth,* the dying can use another person, as is usually the case in the growing process, and direct his libidinal and aggressive emotions to that person. As a phase of growth, dying contains in a nutshell the possibility of solving the various derivatives of the life and death instincts, in a way that enables the dying to part from life and create for himself an image of the future that will satisfy his libidinal need for safety and security when the destructive impulses of the death instinct are aimed at the values of the life he has lived.

A person capable of growth attaches his libido to real, living people. Especially in childhood the interaction with his environment enables him to build new personality structures and ego functions. A dying person, however, attaches his libido either to inner representations of past human relations, or to the transference to the person caring for him, or to fantasies of life after death. In this way libido becomes attached to created objects in the form of illusions. The illusions are equivalent to the emotional reality and the ongoing depth of regression while the personality structure of the dying person grows weaker and is disintegrated.

A dying person also decathects or turns away from objects that are no longer of use to him and that cannot offer constancy to his libido. The sick, dying body, all the skills and abilities he no longer has the power to use, various life-preserving values of his life and family in general, lose their meaning. In very much the same way as a growing person does, the dying person detaches his libido from the object, and the aggressive instinctual impulses are directed to the object without the former fusion of libido and aggression. As a consequence of the defusion, the inner representations of the objects of libidinal interest are destroyed and vanish from the mind of the dying person. The dying person's cathexis is instead directed first toward objects that he has reason to believe will carry on his existence in the form of auxiliary egos, second toward the therapist caring for him, and third toward his fantasies of death or of the life after death.

Thus far dying follows the pattern of growth without being an actual process of growth with ensuing progress in the development of personality and ego functions. Similarly, fantasies of death conform to various familiar patterns of life. The fantasies and the auxiliary egos of the dying person are as free as possible of aggression, perhaps for the very reason that they are fantasies and have not been molded in real interaction between subject and object. The image thus created of a state of peace and rest where there is no emotional ambivalence, and where aggressive impulses do not destroy the created illusions, is based on the imaginary quality of fantasy and not on experiences of real life.

Theological and theological-philosophical models of thinking have often sought to deny the destructive nature of the death instinct, i.e., to deny the fact that something is actually destroyed when a new structure, a new function, or a new cathectic constellation is created. The theological-philosophical conceptions of a heavenly state of being, of Nirvana, or of a general state of peace or individual striving to attain such a state, correspond neither to biological nor to psychic patterns of growth. The fantasy of a peaceful state or of striving to reach such a state does, however, correspond to a dying person's wish to attain a state where there would be only libidinal aims, and the destructive impulses of the death instinct would support libidinal impulses only in order to make death but a gateway for new life for the person.

Enduring the death process of another person as an object of both his libidinal and aggressive instinctual impulses,

either in a real human relationship or in a transference relationship, can be easier if we are able to understand that the
dying needs another person not only as a defense against the
fear of death but also and most of all as a human relation so
as to be able to die in a creative way in accordance with the
pattern of growth.

References

Achté, K. A. & Vauhkonen, M.-L. (1967a), Cancer and the psyche. *Ann. Med. Intern. Fenn.*, 56, Suppl. 49.
—————————— (1967b), Syöpä ja psyyke. [Cancer and the psyche.] *Duodecim*, 83:678-685.
Alexander, I. E. & Adelstein, A. M. (1965), Affective responses to the concept of death in a population of children and early adolescents. In: *Death and Identity*, ed. R. Fulton. New York: Wiley, pp. 111-123.
Altschul, S. (1968), Denial and ego arrest. *J. Amer. Psychoanal. Assn.*, 16:301-318.
Aronsen, G. J. (1959), Treatment of the dying person. In: *The Meaning of Death*, ed. H. Feifel. New York: McGraw-Hill, pp. 251-258.
Barnes, M. J. (1964), Reactions to the death of a mother. *The Psychoanalytic Study of the Child*, 19:334-357. New York: International Universities Press.
Bowlby, J. (1960), Grief and mourning in infancy and early childhood. *The Psychoanalytic Study of the Child*, 15:9-52. New York: International Universities Press.
Brodsky, B. (1959), Liebestod fantasies in a patient faced with a fatal illness. *Internat. J. Psycho-Anal.*, 40:13-16.
Bromberg, W. & Schilder, P. (1936), The attitude of psychoneurotics toward death. *Psychoanal. Rev.*, 23:1-25.
Browne, I. W. & Hackett, T. P. (1967), Emotional reactions to the threat of impending death. *Irish J. Med. Sci.*, 6:177-187.
Cappon, D. (1961), The psychology of dying. In: *Death: Interpretations*, ed. H. M. Ruitenbeek. New York: Dell, 1969, pp. 61-72.
Christ, A. E. (1965), Attitudes towards death among a group of acute geriatric psychiatric patients. In: *Death and Identity*, ed. R. Fulton. New York: Wiley, pp. 146-152.
Deutsch, F. (1935), Euthanasia: A clinical study. *Psychoanal. Quart.*, 5:347-368, 1936.
Deutsch, H. (1937), Absence of grief. *Psychoanal. Quart.*, 6:12-22.

247

Easson, W. M. (1968), Care of the young patient who is dying. *J. Amer. Med. Assn.,* 205:203-207.

Eidelberg, L. (1959), The concept of narcissistic mortification. *Internat. J. Psycho-Anal.,* 40:163-168.

Eissler, K. R. (1955), *The Psychiatrist and the Dying Patient.* New York: International Universities Press.

——— (1963), *Goethe: A Psychoanalytic Study.* Detroit, Mich.: Wayne State University Press.

——— (1972), Death drive, ambivalence, and narcissism. *The Psychoanalytic Study of the Child,* 26:25-78. New York: Quadrangle.

Enckell, O. (1961), *Edith Södergran's Dikter I och II.* [*Edith Södergran's Poetry I and II.*] Helsinki: Svenska Litteratursällskapet i Finland. [Swedish Literature Society.]

Erikson, E. H. (1951), Sex differences in the play configurations of a representative group of pre-adolescents. *Amer. J. Orthopsychiat.,* 21:667-692.

——— (1958), *Young Man Luther: A Study in Psychoanalysis and History.* New York: Norton.

——— (1968), Womanhood and the inner space. *Identity: Youth and Crisis.* New York: Norton, pp. 261-294.

Feifel, H. (1959), Attitudes toward death in some normal and mentally ill populations. In: *The Meaning of Death,* ed. H. Feifel. New York: McGraw-Hill, pp. 114-130.

Fenichel, O. (1945), *The Psychoanalytic Theory of Neurosis.* New York: Norton.

Freud, A. (1922), Beating fantasies and daydreams. *The Writings of Anna Freud,* 1:137-157. New York: International Universities Press, 1974.

——— (1952), The mutual influences in the development of ego and id: Introduction to the discussion. *The Writings of Anna Freud,* 4:230-244. New York: International Universities Press, 1968.

——— (1960), Discussion of Dr. John Bowlby's work on separation, grief and mourning, Part II. *The Writings of Anna Freud,* 5:173-186. New York: International Universities Press, 1969.

——— (1965), Normality and pathology in childhood: Assessments of development. *The Writings of Anna Freud,* 6. New York: International Universities Press.

——— (1967), About losing and being lost. *The Writings of Anna Freud,* 4:302-316. New York: International Universities Press, 1968.

——— & Burlingham, D. (1944), Infants without families. *The Writings of Anna Freud,* 3:543-666. New York: International Universities Press, 1973.

Freud, S. (1900), The interpretation of dreams. *Standard Edition,* 4. London: Hogarth Press, 1953.

——— (1905), Three essays on the theory of sexuality. *Standard Edition,* 7:130-243. London: Hogarth Press, 1959.

_____ (1908a), Creative writers and day-dreaming. *Standard Edition,* 9:143-153. London: Hogarth Press, 1959.

_____ (1908b), On the sexual theories of children. *Standard Edition,* 9:209-226. London: Hogarth Press, 1959.

_____ (1910), Leonardo da Vinci and a memory of his childhood. *Standard Edition,* 11:63-137. London: Hogarth Press, 1957.

_____ (1911), Formulations on the two principles of mental functioning. *Standard Edition,* 12:218-226. London: Hogarth Press, 1958.

_____ (1913), Totem and taboo. *Standard Edition,* 13:1-162. London: Hogarth Press, 1955.

_____ (1914), On narcissism. *Standard Edition,* 14:73-102. London: Hogarth Press, 1957.

_____ (1915), Thoughts for the times on war and death, Part II: Our attitude towards death. *Standard Edition,* 14:289-300. London: Hogarth Press, 1957.

_____ (1917), Mourning and melancholia. *Standard Edition,* 14:243-258. London: Hogarth Press, 1957.

_____ (1920), Beyond the pleasure principle. *Standard Edition,* 18:7-64. London: Hogarth Press, 1955.

_____ (1921), Group psychology and the analysis of the ego. *Standard Edition,* 18:69-143. London: Hogarth Press, 1955.

_____ (1923), The ego and the id. *Standard Edition,* 19:12-59. London: Hogarth Press, 1961.

_____ (1924), The dissolution of the Oedipus complex. *Standard Edition,* 19:173-179. London: Hogarth Press, 1961.

_____ (1926a), Inhibitions, symptoms and anxiety. *Standard Edition,* 20:87-172. London: Hogarth Press, 1959.

_____ (1926b), The question of lay analysis. *Standard Edition,* 20:183-258. London: Hogarth Press, 1959.

_____ (1928), Dostoevsky and parricide. *Standard Edition,* 21:177-194. London: Hogarth Press, 1961.

_____ (1940), An outline of psycho-analysis. *Standard Edition,* 23:144-207. London: Hogarth Press, 1964.

Furman, R. A. (1964a), Death and the young child. *The Psychoanalytic Study of the Child,* 19:321-333. New York: International Universities Press.

_____ (1964b), Death of a six-year-old's mother during his analysis. *The Psychoanalytic Study of the Child,* 19:377-397. New York: International Universities Press.

Greenacre, P. (1957), The childhood of the artist: Libidinal phase development and giftedness. *Emotional Growth,* Vol. 2. New York: International Universities Press, 1971, pp. 479-504.

_____ (1958), The family romance of the artist. *Emotional Growth,* Vol. 2. New York: International Universities Press, 1971, pp. 505-532.

———— (1960), Woman as artist. *Emotional Growth*, Vol. 2. New York: International Universities Press, 1971, pp. 575-591.

Greenberger, E. (1965), Fantasies of women confronting death. *J. Consult. Psychol.*, 29:252-260.

Hägglund, T.-B. (1973), Lapsi ja kuolema [Child and death] *Duodecim*, 89:1161-1167.

———— (1974), Luovasta lukemisesta ja kirjoittamisesta. [On creative reading and writing.] Mielenterveys, 6:23.

———— (1977), On development and growth. *Psychiat. Fenn.*, pp. 41-46.

———— & Hägglund, V. (1970), Kuolevan potilaan psykoterapia [Psychotherapy of a dying patient.] *Suom. Lääk. Lehti*, 25:1825-1832.

Hartmann, H. (1964), *Essays on Ego Psychology*. New York: International Universities Press.

Hauser, A. (1958), *The Philosophy of Art History*. New York: Knopf.

Hinton, J. (1967), *Dying*. Aylesbury, Eng.: Hunt Barnard.

Horney, K. (1926), The flight from womanhood. *Internat. J. Psycho-Anal.*, 7:324-339.

———— (1932), The dread of woman. *Internat. J. Psycho-Anal.*, 13:348-360.

Horton, P. C. (1974), The mystical experience: Substance of an illusion. *Amer. J. Psychoanal. Assn.*, 22:364-380.

Jacobson, E. (1950), Development of the wish for a child in boys. *The Psychoanalytic Study of the Child*, 5:139-152. New York: International Universities Press.

Jaques, E. (1965), Death and the mid-life crisis. *Internat. J. Psycho-Anal.*, 46:502-514.

Joffe, W. G. & Sandler, J. (1965), Notes on pain, depression, and individuation. *The Psychoanalytic Study of the Child*, 20:394-424. New York: International Universities Press.

———— ———— (1967), On the concept of pain, with special reference to depression and psychogenic pain. *J. Psychosom. Res.*, 11:69-75.

Jones, E. (1933), The phallic phase. *Papers on Psychoanalysis*, 5th ed. London: Bailliere, Tindall & Cox, 1950, pp. 452-484.

Joseph, F. (1962), Transference and countertransference in the case of a dying patient. *Psychoanal. & Psychoanal. Rev.*, 49(4):21-34.

Kemppinen, I. (1967), *Haudantakainen elämä Karjalaisen Muinaisuskon ja Vertailevan Uskontotieteen Valossa*. [*Life beyond Death in the Light of Ancient Carelian Beliefs and the Comparative Theological Sciences.*] Helsinki: Karjalan Tutkimusseura [Carelian Research Society].

Kernberg, O. F. (1974), Further contributions to the treatment of narcissistic personalities. *Internat. J. Psycho-Anal.*, 55:215-240.

Klein, M. (1928), Early stages of the Oedipus conflict. *Contributions to Psycho-Analysis*. London: Hogarth Press, 1948, pp. 202-214.

———— (1948), *Contributions to Psycho-Analysis*. London: Hogarth Press.

Kohut, H. (1971), *The Analysis of the Self.* New York: International Universities Press.

Kris, E. (1952), *Psychoanalytic Explorations in Art.* New York: International Universities Press.

―――― (1953), Psychoanalysis and the study of creative imagination. *Selected Papers.* New Haven: Yale University Press, 1975, pp. 473-493.

Kubie, L. S. (1958), *Neurotic Distortion of the Creative Process.* Lawrence: University of Kansas Press.

Leeuw, P. J. van der (1958), On the preoedipal phase of the male. *Internat. J. Psycho-Anal.,* 39:112-115.

Lesche, C. & Stjernholm-Madsen, E. (1976), *Psykoanalysens Videnskabsteori. Psykologi og Videnskabsteori.* [*The Scientific Theory of Psychoanalysis. Psychology and Scientific Theory.*] Copenhagen: Munksgaard.

LeShan, L. & LeShan, E. (1961), Psychotherapy in the patient with a limited life-span. *Psychiatry,* 24:319-323.

Levin, R. (1964), Truth versus illusion in relation to death. *Psychoanal. Rev.,* 51:190-200.

Mahler, M. S. (1968), *On Human Symbiosis and the Vicissitudes of Individuation.* New York: International Universities Press.

McClelland, D. C. (1964), *The Roots of Consciousness.* Princeton, N.J.: Van Nostrand.

Meyer, B. C. & Blacher, R. S. (1960), The creative impulse―biologic and artistic aspects: Report of a case. *The Psychoanalytic Study of Society,* 1:251-271. New York: International Universities Press.

Milner, M. (1957), *On Not Being Able to Paint.* New York: International Universities Press.

Modell, A. H. (1970), The transitional object and the creative act. *Psychoanal. Quart.,* 39:240-250.

Muensterberger, W. (1962), The creative process: Its relation to object loss and fetishism. *The Psychoanalytic Study of Society,* 2:161-185. New York: International Universities Press.

Munroe, R. L. (1955), *Schools of Psychoanalytic Thought.* New York: Dryden.

Nagera, H. (1970), Children's reactions to the death of important objects. *The Psychoanalytic Study of the Child,* 25:360-400. New York: International Universities Press.

Norton, J. (1963), Treatment of a dying patient. *The Psychoanalytic Study of the Child,* 18:541-560. New York: International Universities Press.

Olsson, H. (1949), *Inledning till Edith Södergran, Samlade Dikter.* [*An Introduction to Edith Södergran's Collected Poems.*] Helsinki: Schildts Förlag.

―――― (1955), *Ediths Brev.* [*Edith's Letters.*] Helsinki: Schildts Förlag.

Papageorgis, D. (1966), On the ambivalence of death; the case of the missing harlequin. *Psychol. Rep.,* 19:325-326.

Parkes, C. M. (1972), Components of the reactions to loss of a limb, spouse or home. *J. Psychosom. Res.*, 16:343-349.

Pfister, O. (1930), Schockdenken und Schockphantasien bei höchster Todesgefahr. *Internat. Z. Psychoanal.*, 16:430-455.

Pollock, G. H. (1961), Mourning and adaptation. *Internat. J. Psycho-Anal.*, 42:341-361.

Rosenthal, H. R. (1957), Psychotherapy for the dying. In: *Death: Interpretations*, ed. H. M. Ruitenbeek. New York: Dell, 1969, pp. 87-95.

Sachs, H. (1942), *The Creative Unconscious*. Cambridge, Mass: Sci-Art.

Sandford, B. (1952), An obsessional man's need to be "kept." *Internat. J. Psycho-Anal.*, 33:144-152.

———— (1957), Some notes on a dying patient. *Internat. J. Psycho-Anal.*, 38:158-165.

Saul, L. J. (1959), Reactions of a man to natural death. *Psychoanal. Quart.*, 28:383-386.

Schafer, R. (1974), Problems in Freud's psychology of women. *J. Amer. Psychoanal. Assn.*, 22:459-485.

Shambaugh, B. (1961), A study of loss reactions in a seven-year-old. *The Psychoanalytic Study of the Child*, 16:510-522. New York: International Universities Press.

Södergran, E. (1966), *Samlade Dikter*. [*Collected Poems.*] Helsinki: Schildts Förlag.

Stekel, W. (1927-1928), *Compulsion and Doubt*. New York: Liveright, 1949.

Stern, M. M. (1968), Fear of death and neurosis. *J. Amer. Psychoanal. Assn.*, 16:3-31.

Stokes, A. D. (1966), On being taken out of oneself. *Internat. J. Psycho-Anal.*, 47:523-530.

Swenson, W. M. (1965), Attitude toward death among the aged. In: *Death and Identity*, ed. R. Fulton. New York: Wiley, pp. 105-111.

Tideström, G. (1949), *Edith Södergran*. Helsinki: Schildts Förlag.

Verwoert, A. & Elmore, J. L. (1967), Psychosocial reactions in fatal illness. I. The prospect of impending death. *J. Amer. Geriat. Soc.*, 15:9-19.

Waelder, R. (1960), *Basic Theory of Psychoanalysis*. New York: International Universities Press.

Wahl, C. W. (1965), The fear of death. In: *Death and Identity*, ed. R. Fulton. New York: Wiley, pp. 56-66.

Weisman, A. D. & Hackett, T. P. (1961), Predilection to death. *Psychosom. Med.*, 23:232-256.

Weissman, P. (1971), The artist and his objects. *Internat. J. Psycho-Anal.*, 52:401-406.

Wind, E. de (1968), The confrontation with death. *Internat. J. Psycho-Anal.*, 49:302-305.

Winnicott, D. W. (1953), Transitional objects and transitional phenomena. *Playing and Reality*. London: Tavistock, 1971, pp. 1-25.

_____ (1954), The depressive position in normal emotional development. *Collected Papers.* London: Tavistock, 1958, pp. 262-277.

_____ (1958), The capacity to be alone. *The Maturational Processes and the Facilitating Environment.* New York: International Universities Press, 1965, pp. 29-36.

_____ (1960), The theory of the parent-infant relationship. *The Maturational Processes and the Facilitating Environment.* New York: International Universities Press, 1965, pp. 37-55.

_____ (1971), Creativity and its origins. *Playing and Reality.* London: Tavistock, pp. 65-85.

_____ (1974), Fear of breakdown. *Internat. Rev. Psycho-Anal.,* 1:103-107.

Wolf, A. W. M. (1958), *Helping Your Child to Understand Death.* New York: Child Study Association.

Wolfenstein, M. (1965), Death of a parent and death of a president. In: *Children and the Death of a President,* ed. M. Wolfenstein & G. Kliman. New York: Doubleday, pp. 62-79.

_____ (1966), How is mourning possible? *The Psychoanalytic Study of the Child,* 21:93-123. New York: International Universities Press.

Index